S0-BYD-152

950

Money and
Mathematics

PRENTICE HALL GENERAL REFERENCE
15 Columbus Circle
New York, New York 10023

Copyright © 1993 by Merlion Publishing Ltd.

All rights reserved, including the right of reproduction in whole or in part in any form.

PRENTICE HALL and colophon are registered trademarks of Simon & Schuster Inc.

ISBN 0–671–84695–7

Designed by Jane Brett, Steven Hulbert
Manufactured in Great Britain by BPCC Hazells Ltd

Originally published in Great Britain by Merlion Publishing Ltd. as
THE ILLUSTRATED DICTIONARY OF MONEY AND MATHEMATICS in a different form.

A Prentice Hall Illustrated Dictionary

Money and Mathematics

Contributors
Mike Nugent
Jenifer Fellows

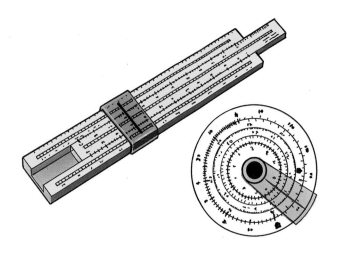

PRENTICE HALL GENERAL REFERENCE

New York · London · Toronto · Sydney · Tokyo · Singapore

Reader's notes

The entries in this dictionary have several features to help you broaden your understanding of the word you are looking up.

- Each entry is introduced by its headword. All the headwords in the dictionary are arranged in alphabetical order.

- Each headword is followed by a part of speech to show whether the word is used as a noun, adjective, verb, or prefix.

- Each entry begins with a sentence that uses the headword as its subject.

- Words that are bold in an entry are cross references. You can look them up in this dictionary to find out more information about the topic.

- The sentence in italics at the end of an entry helps you to see how the headword can be used.

- Many of the entries are accompanied by illustrations. The labels on the illustrations highlight the key points of information and will help you to understand some of the science behind the entries.

- Many of the labels on the illustrations have their own entries in the dictionary and can therefore be used as cross references.

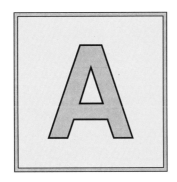

abacus   *noun*
An abacus is a device used for **counting** and doing **arithmetic**. The abacus was invented thousands of years ago and is still in use today. **Multiplication** is done by repeated **addition**, and **division** is done by repeated **subtraction**.
A skilled person can do arithmetic very quickly on an abacus.

account   *noun*
1. An account is a record of **financial transactions**. **Businesses** keep a set of accounts in a book or on a **computer**, in which they record **money** they have paid or are due to **pay**. An account also records money **received** or due to be received.
A fixed asset account contains details of fixed assets bought by a business.
2. An account is an arrangement by which a **customer** can **buy goods** on **credit** from a **supplier**. The customer may be an individual or a business.
He opened an account with Giant Stores.
3. A **bank** account is an arrangement by which a customer leaves money with a bank and then **withdraws** the money when it is needed.
Money held in a bank account often earns interest for its owner.
4. Accounts are **statements** recording the **profit earned** by a business, the **assets** owned by the business and the **liabilities** owed by the business. They are usually prepared at regular intervals, perhaps once a **year**.
The accounts of the company show a profit of $3 million earned last year.

accountant   *noun*
An accountant is a person who prepares the **accounts** of a **business** or an individual **client**. The accountant gathers together all the **financial** information and prepares a summary of the **income** and **expenditure**. An accountant may also provide other **services**, such as advice on **taxes**.
The accountant completed her work on her client's accounts for last year.

acre   *noun*
An acre is an **imperial** unit of **area** used to **measure** land. It is equal to 43,560 **square feet**, or 4,047 square **meters**.
The farmer plowed five acres of land last week.

acute angle   *noun*
An acute angle is an **angle** that is smaller than 90°.
An acute angle makes a sharp point.

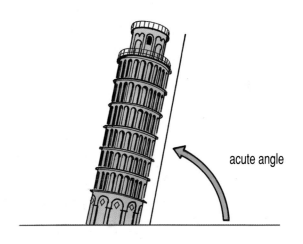

acute angle

addition   *noun*
Addition is a kind of **arithmetic**. It is used to find the total, or **sum**, of two or more **numbers** added together. The sign for addition is +. If there are five cars and six trucks, then addition is used to work out that there are eleven vehicles altogether.
At the supermarket we use addition to find out the cost of our shopping.
add   verb

adjacent angles   *plural noun*
Adjacent angles are two **angles** that meet at the same **point**, or **vertex**, and that have one side in common.
The adjacent angles measured 26° and 13°.

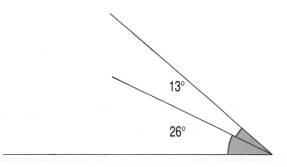

13°
26°

advance   *noun*
An advance is a **sum** of **money paid** by a **customer** before receiving any **goods** or **services**. For example, a **business** might make advance **payments** to the **company** constructing its new offices. An advance is similar to a **deposit**.
The contract was worth $2 million, and the builder asked for an advance of $200,000.
advance   *verb*

afghani   *noun*
The afghani is the **currency** of Afghanistan. An afghani is made up of 100 puls.

algebra   *noun*
Algebra is a kind of **arithmetic**. It is a way of working out **number problems** using both letters and numbers. The letters can stand for an unknown number. Algebra is used to work out an **equation**, such as $y = 2x + 7$.
He used algebra to work out where the rocket would land.
algebraic   *adjective*

algorithm   *noun*
An algorithm is a list of all the processes that need to be carried out to **solve** a **problem**. Algorithms are used in **computer** programs because they tell the computer exactly what to do in the correct order.
She used an algorithm to work out the position of the satellite.

alloy   *noun*
An alloy is a metal made up of two or more metals that have been mixed together. A combination of copper and zinc makes the alloy brass. Alloys are usually harder, lighter in **weight**, and stronger than the metals from which they are made.
The car had lightweight alloy wheels.

alternate angle   *noun*
An alternate angle is an **angle** made when two **lines** are crossed by another **straight line**.
Alternate angles are always the same size.

altitude   *noun*
1. Altitude is another word for **height**. It is usually used to describe how high something is above sea level.
It is difficult to breathe at high altitudes.
2. Altitude in **geometry** is a **line** drawn downward from a **vertex** that is **perpendicular** to the opposite side or face of a **shape**.
A line from the apex of a triangle straight down to the base is the altitude of the triangle.

All three lines measure the altitude of the triangle

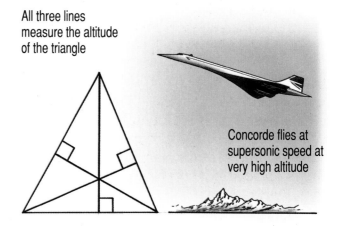

Concorde flies at supersonic speed at very high altitude

A.M.   *abbreviation*
A.M., or a.m., stands for *ante meridiem,* the Latin words meaning "before noon." Six a.m. means six o'clock in the morning.
His plane left at nine a.m

analog *adjective*
Analog describes a system of measurement that shows time, temperature, etc., by numbers on a dial, moving hands, etc. The opposite of analog is digital.
His analog watch had hands, which moved around the dial.

analysis *noun*
In **business**, analysis means the study of a **company's accounts** to decide how healthy it is in **financial** terms. In most cases, the analysis is used to decide whether it is worth **investing** in a company.
She asked an accountant to do an analysis of the company's accounts.

angle ► page 8

angle of depression *noun*
The angle of depression of an object is the **angle** between a **horizontal line** and a line to a **point** below it.
The angle of depression of the beach from the top of the cliff was 350°.

angle of elevation *noun*
The angle of elevation of an object is the **angle** between a **horizontal line** and a line to a **point** above it.
The angle of elevation from the ground to the top of the tree was 90°.

annual *adjective*
Annual describes something that happens once a **year** or that is **calculated** for an entire year. For example, a person's **salary** is usually **computed** on an annual basis.
The tax official looked at the company's annual accounts.

annual percentage rate ► APR

annuity *noun*
1. An annuity is a **sum** of money that is **paid** to a person every **year**.
The company gives their employees an annuity when they retire.

2. An annuity is a kind of **investment** that earns a yearly **income** that is paid to the investor.
The annuity paid an income of $1,000 every year for ten years.

ante meridiem ► **A.M.**

apex *noun*
The apex of an object is the highest **point** it reaches above its **base**.
The apex of a mountain is its highest peak.

approximation *noun*
An approximation is a **number** or a **value** that is a close guess but that may not be exact. An approximation is normally close enough to be acceptable.
If there are 499 beads in a box, an approximation of the total would be 500.
approximately *adverb*

APR *abbreviation*
APR is short for annual percentage rate. APR is the **annual interest** that is to be **paid** on a **loan**. Banks generally **charge** interest for every **month** that a loan is not **repaid**. The APR denotes the interest that would be paid over a whole year.
To decide which loan is cheapest, compare the APRs offered by each bank.

angle   *noun*

An angle is the point where two lines or surfaces meet. The angle between two lines measures how much one line turns away from the other. Angles are measured in degrees with a **protractor**. They are grouped under particular names depending on how great the angle is.

At three o'clock, the angle between the hour hand and the minute hand measures 90°.

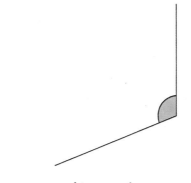

obtuse angle
an angle greater than 90° but less than 180°

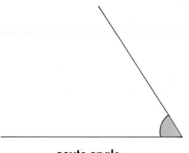

acute angle
an angle greater than 0° but less than 90°

straight angle
an angle of 180°

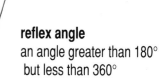

reflex angle
an angle greater than 180° but less than 360°

right angle
an angle of 90°

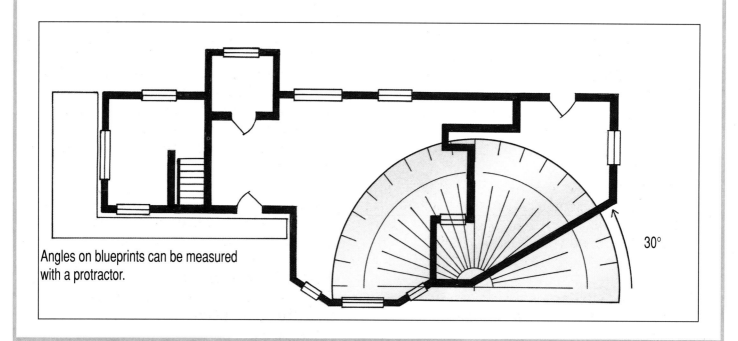

Angles on blueprints can be measured with a protractor.

30°

8

arc   *noun*
An arc is a section of the **circumference** of a **circle**, or part of a **curve**. A pair of **compasses** can be used to draw regular arcs.
A semicircle is an arc, and so is any portion of the letter S.

area   *noun*
Area is the amount of flat space something takes up on a **surface**. Area is **measured** in **square units**, such as square **miles** or square **yards**.
The area of the garden was 400 square feet.

arithmetic   *noun*
Arithmetic is a way of **solving problems** with **numbers**. Arithmetic uses **addition, subtraction, multiplication**, and **division**.
Arithmetic was used to figure out how much money had been spent.

assay   *noun*
An assay is a test of a metal to see what it contains. It is used to test **gold** and **silver coins** or **bullion** to see how pure they are.
The assay showed that the coin contained 2 grams of gold.

asset   *noun*
An asset is an item of **value** owned by a **business** or an individual. **Money**, machines, and buildings are all assets. Assets and **liabilities** are listed on the **balance sheet** of a business.
The value of some assets can be hard to determine.

associative   *adjective*
Associative describes an operation in which the way the elements are grouped does not change the result. For example, in addition, $1 + (2 + 3) = 6$, and $(1 + 2) + 3 = 6$. In multiplication, $2 \times (2 \times 2) = 8$, and $(2 \times 2) \times 2 = 8$.
Division and subtraction are not associative.
Multiplication and addition are both associative.

asymmetrical   *adjective*
Asymmetrical describes an object or **design** that has no **symmetry**. There is no way to **divide** it so that one half is equal in **shape** and **size** to the other half.
F, G, and J are all letters that have an asymmetrical shape.

auction   *noun*
An auction is a form of public **sale** where **goods** are offered without a set **price**. Each item is sold to the person who offers the most **money**.
The cattle were sold to local farmers at the auction.

audit   *noun*
An audit is a check on the **accounts** of a **company**. The audit is carried out by a person from outside the company, usually an **accountant**. In many countries, companies are required by law to have their accounts audited each **year**. The person who does the audit is called an auditor.
The audit revealed no major errors in the accounts.

austral   *noun*
The austral is the **currency** of Argentina. An austral is made up of 100 australes.

Australian dollar   *noun*
The Australian dollar is the **currency** of Australia. The Australian dollar is made up of 100 cents.

automation *noun*
Automation is a way in which **computers** are designed to do work instead of people. Computers can be programmed to do many **jobs** that might be boring or dangerous for human beings. **Factories** are now being built where **goods** are **manufactured** automatically, but people are still needed to check that **products** are made properly.
Robots are used in automation.

average *noun*
An average is a **number** found by **adding** several **values** together and then **dividing** the total by the number of values. The average of 3, 7, 14, and 16 is 3 + 7 + 14 + 16 ÷ 4 = 10. Another word for average is mean.
The batsman scored an average of 42 runs.

axis (plural **axes**) *noun*
1. An axis is a **line** on a **graph**. The vertical axis, called the y-axis, is **vertical**. The horizontal axis, called the x-axis, is **horizontal**.
The vertical axis showed the weight of the bricks.
2. An axis of **symmetry** is a line that cuts a **shape** into two equal, matching parts.
The diameter is an axis of symmetry of a circle.
3. An axis of rotation is a line that a **solid** body can turn around. The axis of **Earth** is an imaginary line running between the North Pole and the South Pole.
The Earth turns on its axis once every 24 hours.

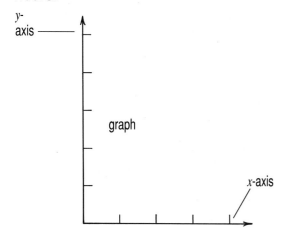

B

baht *noun*
The baht is the **currency** of Thailand. The baht is made up of 100 satang.

balance *noun*
1. The balance is an amount of **money** in an **account**. A balance can be either money owed or money available.
The balance of the bank account was $250.
2. A balance is a device used to measure the weight of something.
The grocer weighed the vegetables on the balance.

balance of payments *noun*
The balance of payments is an **account** totaling all the **payments** made by a country to other countries, and all the payments **received** by the country from other countries. A country makes payments in order to **import goods** from other countries. It receives payments if it **exports** goods. If a country's exports are high and its imports are low, it has a positive balance of payments. If its imports are high and its exports are low, it has a negative, or adverse, balance of payments.
The balance of payments was negative for the tenth year in a row.

balance of trade   *noun*
The balance of trade is one part of the
balance of payments. It refers to **money
paid** and **received** for **trade** in **goods**. This
kind of trade is known as visible trade.
Invisible trade means trade in **services**,
such as **banking** and **insurance**.
*The balance of trade has improved recently
because exports of consumer goods are
increasing.*

balance sheet ► page 12

bank   *noun*
A bank is a place where people can leave
their **money**. They are the bank's
customers, and each customer has an
account. Customers can get their money
out again by **withdrawing** it or by writing a
check.
Banks also lend money.

banker   *noun*
A banker is a person who manages a **bank**.
The banker loaned 500 dollars to a client.

bank note   *noun*
A bank note is a printed piece of paper that
is issued by a government and that can be
used as **money**. The bank note will be
accepted as **legal tender**, which means that
everyone who handles it accepts its **face
value**. Bank notes are intricately printed to
prevent **forgery**.
*The bank notes in the wallet added up to 25
dollars.*

bankrupt   *adjective*
Bankrupt describes **companies** or people
who cannot **pay** their **debts**. When a person
or company goes bankrupt, the **creditors** try
to work out an arrangement so they will get
at least some of the **money** that they are
owed.
*The shoe factory went bankrupt when sales
decreased.*
bankruptcy   *noun*

bar chart   *noun*
A bar chart is a **graph** that uses **lines** or
bars to compare the total **value** of several
items. There are two kinds, or styles, of bar
charts – horizontal bar charts and vertical
bar charts.
*The bar chart shows that there are more
size-seven shoes than any other size in
stock.*

bar chart

dozens	1	2	3	4	5	6
7						
6						
5						
4						
3						

bar code   *noun*
A bar code is a pattern of bars and lines that
hold information in **code**. A computer is
used to read the code, which may contain
information on price, quantity, and a
description of the item.
Food packages have a bar code on them.

balance sheet   *noun*

A balance sheet is a statement of the financial affairs of a business as of a certain date. It shows the amount of **capital** and retained **profits**, or reserves, invested in the business. It also shows the **assets** that they have been used to buy, and lists the amounts owed by the business.

A balance sheet is usually prepared by an accountant.

Balance Sheet of The Beautiful Balloon Company as of March 31, 1992

ASSETS	$	$
Fixed Assets (at cost less depreciation):		
Land and buildings		500
Plant and machinery		400
Fixtures and fittings		200
Total fixed assets		$1,100
Current assets:		
Stock	600	
Debtors	500	
Prepayments	100	
Cash	200	
	1,400	
Current liabilities:		
Bank loans	200	
Creditors	300	
	500	
Working capital		900
Total net assets		$2,000
CAPITAL AND RESERVES		
Ordinary shares ($1 each)		1,000
Share premium		500
Reserves		500
Total Capital and Reserves		$2,000

things like desks, chairs and telephones

people the company owes money to

subtract the liabilities from the current assets to give the working capital

the totals of each category always balance

12

bargain *noun*
A bargain is something that is bought for a lower **price** than usual.
A VCR costing only $100 would be a bargain.

bargain *verb*
To bargain is to discuss what the **price** of something will be, or how **payment** will be made.
The customer bargained with the salesperson to try and buy the car more cheaply.

barter *verb*
To barter is to **trade goods** or **services** without using **money**.
The farmer bartered three bushels of apples for four chickens.
barter *noun*

base *noun*
1. The base of a **shape** is its bottom or lowest **line** or **surface**.
The base of the triangle measured eight inches.
2. A base is a system of writing **numbers**. In base 10, numbers are made up of the ten **digits** 0, 1, 2, 3, 4, 5, 6, 7, 8, 9. The **decimal** system uses base 10. In the **binary** system, every number is made up of the digits 0 and 1, so the base is 2.
Computers use base 2.

base pay *noun*
Base pay is a rate of **pay** that is set up, or established, for a particular job. Certain extra amounts of money may be added to the base pay. Examples of these are payments for length of service or for an increase in the cost of living.
Her base pay was increased after she had worked for the company for one year.

bax unit ► **SI unit**

bazaar *noun*
A bazaar is a kind of **market**. It has **shops** and stalls where many different kinds of **goods** are for sale.
Many Middle Eastern towns and cities have bazaars.

bearing *noun*
A bearing is a direction **measured** in **degrees**. It is always the measurement of the **angle** between a **line** running north and south and a second line. The bearing of a ship is the angle between the direction that the ship is sailing in and the direction of the North or South pole.
The ship's bearing is 50° and the plane's bearing is 280°.

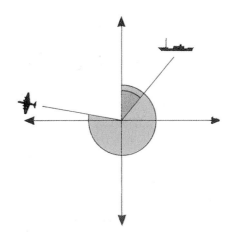

Belgian franc *noun*
The Belgian franc is the **currency** of Belgium. One Belgian franc is made up of 100 centimes.

bet *noun*
A bet is a kind of agreement between two people about an event that is uncertain. For example, if a **coin** is tossed, one person might bet that the coin will show **heads**, and the other person will bet that it will show **tails**. The person who is correct wins the bet.
People often place a bet for money, so that the loser has to pay the winner.
bet *verb*

bid *noun*
A bid is an offer of a **sum** of **money** for something. At an **auction**, anyone wishing to **buy** an item places a bid, according to the amount he or she is willing to **pay**. The item is sold to the person who offers the highest bid.
She bid $4,000 for the picture.

bill *noun*
1. A bill is a list of **prices charged** for work done. For example, an auto mechanic may prepare a bill listing the repair work done on a car and the parts replaced. The total of the **charges** must then be **paid** by the owner of the car. Another word for a bill is an invoice.
The customer was surprised when he saw the amount of the bill.
2. A bill is a document that promises someone a certain amount of **money** to be paid on a particular date. This is often referred to as a bill of exchange.
The bill of exchange was to be paid 90 days after it was issued.

billion *noun*
A billion is a thousand **millions.** It is written 1,000,000,000. In some countries in Europe, a billion is used to mean a million millions (1,000,000,000,000).
The company had sales of 2 billion dollars last year.

billionaire *noun*
A billionaire is a person who has a **billion units** of **currency**. In the United States, a billionaire has a billion **dollars**.
The British billionaire had a billion pounds invested in oil paintings.

bill of lading *noun*
A bill of lading is a list of all the **goods** that are to be transported from one place to another during a single journey.
The ship's captain gave the bill of lading to the customs officer.

binary *adjective*
Binary describes **counting** in **base** 2. Binary counting uses only the two **digits** 0 and 1. In the binary system, 11011 means 1 sixteen, 1 eight, 0 fours, 1 two and 1 **unit**. 11011 in binary is equivalent to 16 + 8 + 0 + 2 + 1 = 27 in base 10.
The binary system is used in digital computers.

bisect *verb*
To bisect is to **divide** into two equal parts. **Lines** and **angles** are bisected when another line is drawn to divide them in half.
The diameter bisects a circle into two equal halves.

bit *noun*
Bit is short for **binary digit**. A bit is a 0 or a 1 that is used in binary **numbers**.
The number 110101 has 6 bits.

1 1 0 1 0 1

black market *noun*
A black market is a way of **selling goods** illegally. Goods may be **rationed**, or sold only in small **quantities**, when they are in short **supply**. Other goods may not be allowed to be sold at all because they are dangerous or rare. However, people may still be able to **buy** these things on the black market.
In Moscow, he bought gasoline on the black market.

block graph *noun*
A block graph is a **graph** that uses **rectangles**, or blocks, to compare the **value** of different items.
He drew a block graph of his exam results.

board of directors ► page 16

boiling point *noun*
The boiling point is the temperature at which a liquid boils. When the temperature is higher than the boiling point, the liquid turns into a gas.
The boiling point of water is 212 degrees Fahrenheit, or 100 degrees Celsius.

bolívar *noun*
The bolívar is the **currency** of Venezuela. One bolívar is made up of 100 centimes.

Bolivian peso *noun*
The Bolivian peso is the **currency** of Bolivia. One Bolivian peso is made up of 100 centavos.

bond *noun*
A bond is a piece of paper that is **issued** by a **company** or a government and bought by individuals or **businesses**. The government or company promises to **repay** the **money** at a certain point in the future. In the meantime it pays **interest** as a reward for the **loan** of the money.
She bought $5,000 worth of bonds, which earned interest throughout the year.

bonus *noun*
A bonus is extra **money paid** as a reward. In some **companies**, people are paid a bonus if they work harder.
Everyone was paid a bonus for selling more toys than in the previous month.

bookkeeping *noun*
Bookkeeping is a system of recording the **transactions** of a **business** by making entries in **books of account**. It is usual to use two entries to describe any transaction, and the term double entry bookkeeping is often used. Nowadays, bookkeeping is often done on a **computer**, with no real books being used.
The company's bookkeeping system was fully computerized.

Date	Received From	Amount $	Date	Paid To	Amount $
Dec 12	Mr Brown	98.50	Dec 1	dairy	6.00
			Dec 1	Mr White	12.00
Dec 16	Mr Green	1,300.00	Dec 2	petty cash	5.00
			Dec 10	salary	65.00
			Dec 11	post office	4.60
Dec 21	Mrs Black	3,000.00	Dec 17	salary	65.00
			Dec 22	Paper Ltd	125.00
				Film Ltd	600.00
				telephone	300.00
				salary	130.00

board of directors *noun*

A board of directors is a group of people who manage the **business** of a **company**. They hold regular meetings, called board meetings, to discuss **policy** and make decisions about what the company should be doing. Each member of the board usually represents one particular branch, or department of the business, such as sales, personnel or distribution.

The board of directors of Superco Inc. meet every month.

books of account *plural noun*
Books of account are all the records kept by a **company** to describe its **financial** activities. For example, **sales** made to **customers** may be recorded in a **cash book**. This is one of the company's books of account.
Books of account are written up regularly so that all the transactions of a company are recorded.

borrow *verb*
To borrow means to obtain **money** that has to be **repaid** in the future. People often borrow money from **banks**. Until the money is repaid, the person who borrows usually has to pay **interest**.
The sailor will borrow $10,000 to buy a new boat.

borrower *noun*
A borrower is someone who **borrows money**.
The borrower paid interest each month until the money was repaid.

bottom line *noun*
The bottom line is slang for the profits or losses of a **business** over a certain period. This term is used because the profit or loss is shown on the lowest line of a company's earnings report.
The corporation's bottom line showed a small profit for the year.

bounce *verb*
To bounce a **check** means to return it because there is not enough money in the **account**.
The check bounced because he forgot to make the deposit into his account.

Bourse *noun*
The Bourse is the name of the **stock exchange** in Paris, France. *Bourse* is the French word for "purse."
The stock of the French company was listed on the Bourse.

brand *noun*
A brand is a kind of **trademark**. It is the name that a **company** gives to one of its **products**. A brand is also a certain kind, grade, or make of **goods**.
The store sold many different brands of soap powder.
brand *verb*

breadth *noun*
Breadth is another word for width. It is the **measurement** of **distance** from one side of something to the other.
He measured the breadth of the football field.
broad *adjective*

broker *noun*
A broker is a person who **buys** and **sells** things on behalf of other people. A stockbroker buys **stocks** for his or her **customers**. An **insurance** broker arranges insurance for a customer through an insurance company. A broker makes **money** by **charging** a **commission** for his or her **services**.
A real estate broker sells real estate for his or her clients.

budget *noun*
1. A budget is an **estimate** of amounts of **money** expected to be **paid** and **received** during some future period. For example, a **business** will often prepare a budget to set out its **financial** plans for the **year** ahead. Governments also make budgets each year that show their plans for raising money from **taxes**, and **spending** money on such things as roads and hospitals.
The company's budget for next year shows an expected profit of $800,000.
2. A budget is an amount of money set aside for some particular purpose in the future.
A budget of 2 million dollars was set aside for the building project.
budget *verb*
budgetary *adjective*

bullion *noun*
Bullion is bars of **gold** or **silver** before it is made into **coins**.
The United States keeps some of its gold bullion at Fort Knox.

bull market *noun*
Bull market is a term used to describe the **stock market** when **prices** are rising. "Bulls" are **investors** who **buy shares** in the hope that they can **sell** them later on at a higher price.
The investor held onto her shares as the bull market continued.

bureau de change *noun*
A bureau de change is a place where the **currency** of one country can be exchanged for the currency of another country.
The traveller converted 50 French francs to American dollars at the bureau de change.

burglary *noun*
Burglary is the **theft** of **possessions** from a building. A burglary can take place from someone's house, or from an office or a **factory**. Burglary is a crime.
The family lost their television in the burglary.

business *noun*
1. Business is the work that people do. For example, the business of a shopkeeper is to sell things to **customers**.
The company's business is to make computers.

2. A business is an organization set up to **supply goods** or **services** to customers in exchange for **money**. A business may be very small, such as a **trader selling** clothes from a **market** stall. Or it may be very large, like an **international bank**. Most large businesses, and some small ones, are **corporations**.
They set up a business to publish books.

buy *verb*
To buy is to give a **sum** of **money** in exchange for something. People usually buy things at a **store**.
He wanted to buy a new coat.

buyer *noun*
A buyer is someone who **buys** things on behalf of a **business**. For example, a clothes **manufacturer** might **employ** a buyer to **purchase** material used to make the clothes.
The buyer bought enough material for 800 coats.

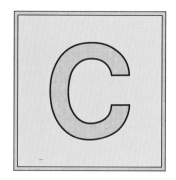

calculation   *noun*
A calculation is a way of **solving** a **number problem**. Calculations can use **addition**, **subtraction**, **multiplication**, and **division** to produce an answer.
The calculation of the profit took a long time.
calculate   *verb*

calculator   *noun*
A calculator is a machine that can do **arithmetic**. For a long time the **abacus** and **slide rule** were used to **solve problems** in arithmetic, but in most countries these devices have been replaced by the electronic calculator.
Some calculators are powered by solar energy.

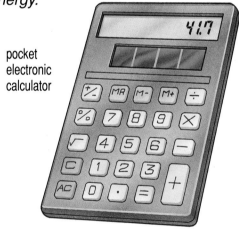

pocket
electronic
calculator

calculus   *noun*
Calculus is a branch of mathematics. It often involves the use of **symbols** from **algebra** to **solve problems** concerned with **statistics** and changing quantities.
The mathematician used calculus to solve the problem.

calendar   *noun*
A calendar is a **table** that shows the **days**, **weeks**, and **months** of a **year**. Many calendars have a space next to each date for recording important information such as appointments and birthdays.
A Hindu calendar is circular and based on lunar months.

Canadian dollar   *noun*
The Canadian dollar is the **currency** of Canada. It is made up of 100 **cents**.

cancel   *verb*
To cancel is to **simplify** a **fraction** down to its lowest form. In canceling, both the **numerator** and **denominator** are divided by the same **number**.
She used canceling to simplify $\frac{4}{20}$ down to $\frac{1}{5}$.

capacity   *noun*
Capacity is a form of **measurement**. It is the amount of space, or **volume**, that something takes up. The main **metric unit** of capacity is the liter.
The capacity of the watering can was 1 gallon.

capital   *noun*
The capital of a **business** is the amount of **money invested** in it. This money is spent to **buy** the things the business needs to carry on its **trade**. For example, capital may be used by a company to buy equipment and buildings.
The corporation sold more stock to raise more capital.

capital gain *noun*
A capital gain is a **profit** earned by **selling** an **asset** for more than it cost to **buy**. Someone might make a capital gain by selling **stock** in a **corporation**. A **company** might make a capital gain by selling a **fixed asset**, such as a **factory**. The opposite of a capital gain is a capital loss.
They made a capital gain when they sold their house for twice the price they paid for it.

capitalism *noun*
Capitalism is a system of **economics** whereby **capital**, or **money**, can be used to develop new **industries** or **services**. In this system people or **companies** can own land, **factories**, or industries to **produce goods** or services for **profit**. The profit can then be reinvested. Capitalism allows companies to **compete** with each other for **trade**.
Capitalism is considered a good system by people who like to make money.

capitalist *noun*
A capitalist is a person who practices capitalism.
Two wealthy capitalists were found to invest money in the failing business.

capital loss ► **capital gain**

cartel *noun*
A cartel is a group of **companies** that agree to work together so that between them they can dominate a **market**. Often the aim of a cartel is to drive other companies out of the market and establish a **monopoly**. In many countries cartels are illegal.
The Organization of Petroleum Exporting Countries, or OPEC, is a cartel of nations that produce oil.

cash *noun*
Cash is **money** in the form of **notes** and **coins**. Money held in a **bank account** is also sometimes referred to as cash.
He had no cash with him so they had to pay by check.

cash book *noun*
A cash book is a record, or **account**, which lists all the **sums** of **cash** it **receives** or **pays**. This includes **payments** by **check** as well as by **notes** and **coins**.
The cash book showed a balance of $100 at the end of the day.

cash card *noun*
A cash card is a small plastic card that is used to **withdraw money** from a **cash dispenser**. The card contains information about the owner's **bank account**, so the cash dispenser can tell which account the money is to be taken from.
A cash card is necessary to withdraw money from a cash dispenser.

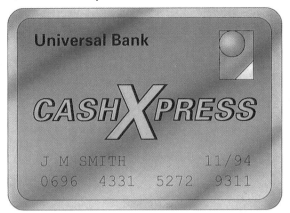

cash dispenser ► page 22

cash flow *noun*
Cash flow is the amount of **money** that comes into and goes out of a **business**.
The company had problems with its cash flow due to low sales.

cash register *noun*
A cash register is a machine used by a **store** to hold and record the **money** people pay for **goods**. It has a keyboard that is used to record the **cash received** from **customers** and a drawer to keep it in. A cash register is often connected to a **computer** that can total the day's **receipts**, as well as keep track of the **inventory**.
The cash register showed that the customer paid cash for the tie.

cash dispenser   *noun*

A cash dispenser is a machine normally operated by a **bank**, from which **customers** can take **money**. The machine is connected to a **compute**r. When a customer puts in a **cash card**, the computer can tell which **account** the money is to be taken from. The customer must type in the correct PIN, or personal identity number, before the computer will release the cash. The computer notes how much money is taken out.

He used the cash dispenser to withdraw $50 from his account.

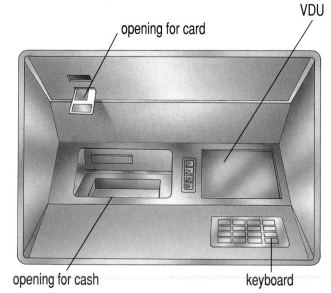

VDU

opening for card

opening for cash

keyboard

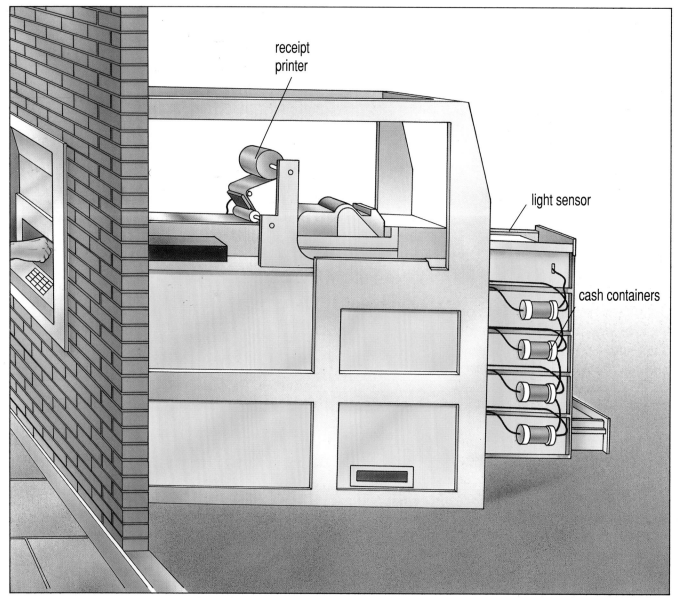

receipt printer

light sensor

cash containers

casino *noun*
A casino is a building where people play games to try to win **money**. This is known as **gambling**. People can play a variety of card games at a casino, including blackjack. Roulette is a game in which a small ball spins around a numbered wheel. Players bet on which **number** the ball will land on when the wheel stops spinning.
Casinos are not legal in most U.S. states and many foreign countries.

Celsius *noun*
Celsius, or centigrade, is a **scale** of temperature from 0° to 100°, where 0° is the **freezing point** of water and 100° is the **boiling point**. The Celsius scale is normally marked on a thermometer
The Celsius scale is named after a Swedish scientist of the same name.

cent *noun*
A cent is one hundredth of a **dollar**.

centi- *prefix*
Centi- is a prefix that means one hundredth. A centimeter is a hundredth of a meter. There are 100 centimeters in a meter.
The cactus was 14 centimeters tall.

centigrade ► **Celsius**

centimeter *noun*
A centimeter is a **measurement** of **length** in the **metric system**. There are 100 centimeters in a meter. About 2.54 centimeters equal one **inch**.
He measured the tabletop in centimeters.

century *noun*
A century is 100 **years**.
His grandfather lived for exactly a century.

chamber of commerce *noun*
A chamber of commerce is an organization that helps **business** people meet and work together in their local area. It also tries to attract outside **clients** to work with local **suppliers**.
The chamber of commerce helped them meet new clients in their town.

chance *noun*
Chance is the likelihood that a specific event will happen. Chance is also used to mean **probability**.
The chance of being struck by lightning is very slim.

change *verb*
To change is to convert from one unit of **currency** to another. For example, U.S. dollars can be changed into French francs or British pounds.
They went to the bureau de change to change their dollars into the local currency.

change *noun*
Change is another word for loose **coins**. It often means the **cash** difference between **money tendered** for a **purchase** and its **price**. Change is handed back to the **customer** by the **seller**.
The candy was 50¢, so she received 50¢ change from her dollar bill.

charge *noun*
A charge is the **price** for providing **goods** or **services**.
Her charge was $20 an hour for the day's work.

charge *verb*
1. To charge is to ask for **payment** in return for providing **goods** or **services**.
He will charge $50 for doing the work.
2. To charge is to offer payment by means of a **credit card**.
The store clerk asked if he would like to pay cash for his purchase, or charge it to his credit card.

chart *noun*
1. A chart is a **table**, **diagram**, or **graph** used to present information in a visual way. Charts can be used to illustrate information such as quantity or value.
The chart shows how many sales the company had made in a year.
2. A chart is a **map** used for navigating in the air or on the water.
The sailor used his chart to find out where dangerous rocks were located.

cheap *adjective*
Cheap describes something that is inexpensive.
The computer was cheap at $500.

check *noun*
A check is a printed piece of paper that orders a **bank** to **pay money** from an **account** held by the owner of the check. The check has the details of the owner's bank account printed on it. An individual or a **business** can use a check either to **withdraw cash** from the bank in the form of **notes** and **coins**, or to pay other people for **goods** or **services supplied**.
The owner of the business paid the employees by check.

Chilean peso *noun*
The Chilean peso is the **currency** of Chile. The Chilean peso is made up of 100 centavos.

chord *noun*
A chord is a **straight line** that joins two **points** on the **circumference** of a **circle**. It does not pass through the center of the circle.
The chord cut the circle into two unequal parts.

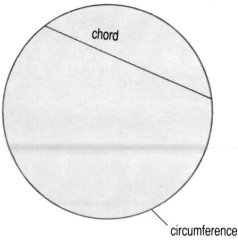

cipher *noun*
A cipher is a secret **code**. **Banks** often use a cipher to send information to other banks. The cipher is used so that if the message reaches the wrong person by accident, it cannot be understood.
The bank manager used a cipher so the message could only be understood by the person to whom it was sent.

circle *noun*
A circle is a round **shape**. The edge or **circumference** of a circle is always the same **distance** from the center **point**.
She drew a circle to show the shape of a wheel.
circular *adjective*

circulation *noun*
Circulation is the way **money** passes from one person to another. For example, when people **buy goods**, they give money to a storekeeper. The storekeeper then uses this money to buy other goods to **sell** and also to **pay** his **employees**. In this way money circulates from one person to another.
The amount of money in circulation changes from year to year.

circumference *noun*
The circumference of a **circle** is the **distance measured** around its edge. If the circumference of a circle is **divided** by the **diameter**, the answer is always the same. This number is called pi and is written π.
The circumference of the circle is 10 inches.

client *noun*
Client is another word for **customer**. Clients **pay** someone else to do a particular **job** for them.
The accountant prepared the annual accounts for each client.

clinometer *noun*
A clinometer **measures** a slope or incline. A clinometer can be used to measure the **angle of elevation** when figuring out the **height** of something.
She used the clinometer to help her calculate the height of a tree.

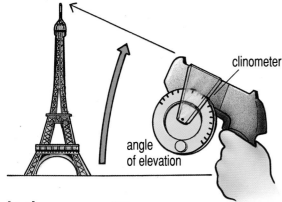

clinometer

angle
of elevation

clock ▶ page 26

clockwise *adjective*
To turn clockwise is to turn in the same direction as the **numbers** and hands of a **clock**.
She remembered to measure the ship's bearing in a clockwise direction.

code *noun*
A code is an arrangement of **symbols** that are used to contain a message. The code may be made up of letters, **numbers**, or a particular graphic.
They used a code to send the message.

coin ▶ page 28

collinear *adjective*
Collinear describes **points** that are located on the same **straight line**.
The points on the graph axis representing days were collinear.

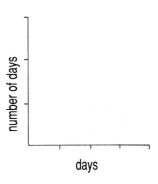

combination *noun*
A combination is a way of grouping **numbers** together. In the **set** of numbers 5, 3, 7, and 4, the numbers can be paired in several different ways: 5,3; 5,7; 5,4; 3,7; 3,4; and 7,4. The **value** of the numbers in a combination does not matter, so 5,3 is considered the same combination as 3,5.
She made different combinations from the numbers 6, 7, 8, and 9.

commerce *noun*
Commerce is the activity in which **goods** and **services** are **bought** and **sold**.
The businessman began in commerce by buying and selling sugar.
commercial adjective

commission *noun*
Commission is a **fee charged** by a person who acts on behalf of some other person or **company**. An **insurance** salesperson earns a commission from the insurance company for each **policy** sold.
The commission was paid to the salesperson after the deal was completed.

clock *noun*

A clock is an instrument for measuring time. There are two main types of clock. Some have pointers, called hands, which turn slowly and point to numbers around the outside of a circular face. Others, known as digital clocks, show a set of numbers on a screen, or readout, that change every minute or second.

The hands on the clock showed half past four.

Ancient Egyptian water clock

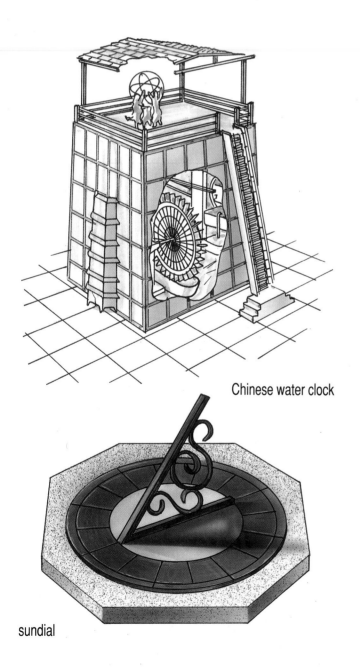

Chinese water clock

candle dial

sundial

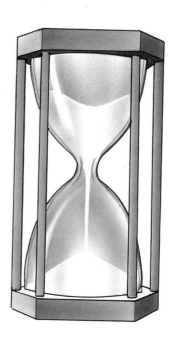

hourglass

pendulum clock

digital watch

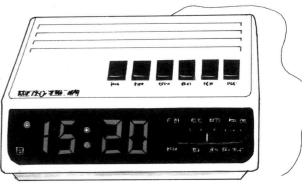

digital clock

coin *noun*

A coin is an item of money made of metal. It is usually of small value only. Money of higher value is issued in the form of **notes**. A coin is usually one of a set. Each coin has a different value relative to a country's main unit of currency. For example, there is a set of six coins in the United States, varying in value from one cent to one dollar. One cent is $\frac{1}{100}$ of a dollar.

The coins in his pocket were worth only about $1.

Gold stater of Philip the Great of Macedon, 350–336 BC.

Hebrew silver shekel, about 1,900 years old.

This brass coin is elegantly fluted.

Scottish 20-pound piece, James VI

Pierced coins are used in some countries.

Maundy money silver penny, George VI.

Retangular coins were used in Japan until the late 1860s.

United Kingdom coins

penny

two pence

five pence

ten pence

twenty pence

fifty pence

one pound

United States coins

cent

five cents (nickel)

ten cents (dime)

twenty-five cents (quarter)

fifty cents (half dollar)

one dollar

commission *verb*
To commission is to ask someone to do a **job** for **payment**.
The company commissioned the artist to paint a picture of the new building.

commodity *noun*
A commodity is something that is **bought** or **sold**. Commodities are often raw materials like wood or iron ore, which will be used to **manufacture** other **goods**. They may also be raw foods, such as sugar cane or coffee beans.
The commodity dealer tried to buy sugar at a very low price.

common denominator *noun*
A common denominator is a **denominator** that is the same for every **fraction** in a group of fractions. In order to be able to **add** or **subtract** a group of fractions, they must all have a common denominator.
She had to work out a common denominator for each fraction so she could add them together.

communications *noun*
Communications includes all the ways of exchanging information.
Computers in a communications network can send messages to each another.

commutative *adjective*
Commutative describes something that can be changed from position to position without altering its **value**. The commutative law means that in **addition** or **multiplication**, the **digits** can be changed from place to place without altering the answer. For example, $3 + 6$ is the same as $6 + 3$. 8×2 is the same as 2×8.
Subtraction and division are not commutative.

company *noun*
A company is another name for a **business**. Some companies are owned by an individual, while others are owned by a group of **investors**. Some are formed into a special type of company called a **corporation**.
After working for the computer manufacturer for ten years, she decided to leave and start her own company.

compass *noun*
1. A compass is a device used to locate the North Pole. It has a **circular** face with north, south, east, and west marked on it and a magnetic needle that always points towards the north.
They used the compass to guide them in a northwest direction.

portable
telephone

2. A compass is an instrument used to draw a **circle**. It has two legs that are joined together so they can open and close. One leg has a point at the end and the other leg holds a pencil.
She drew a circle with the compass.

compensation   *noun*
Compensation is **money paid** to someone either to replace something he or she has lost or as a **salary**. A person who suffers an injury and can no longer work may claim compensation.
He received $20,000 in compensation for his injury.
compensate   *verb*

competition   *noun*
Competition occurs when two or more **companies** try to win the same **customers**. Usually each business will try to give customers better **value** than its competitors. It might **charge** less or make a better **product** so that people will **buy** its **brand**. The opposite of competition is **monopoly**.
Consumers benefit from competition between companies.
compete   *verb*
competitive   *adjective*

complement   *noun*
The complement of a **set** is the collection of all the things that are not part of it. If a basket of fruit contains apples, oranges, and peaches, the complement of the set of apples is the set of oranges and peaches.
The complement can be illustrated on a Venn diagram.

complementary angles   *plural noun*
Complementary angles are two **angles** that add up to 90°.
Angles that measure 60° and 30° are complementary angles.

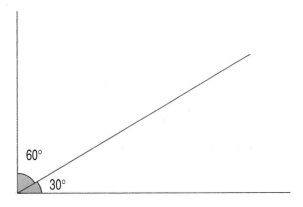

compound interest   *noun*
Compound interest is **interest calculated** on the amount of **money** originally borrowed, plus any interest that has been **added** to this **sum**. It is often **paid** by **banks** on **savings**. If a **loan** is for $100 and the interest **rate** is 10%, the first interest **payment** is calculated on $100, and will be $10. The next interest payment will be calculated on $110, and will be $11.
Compound interest is higher than simple interest.

computer   *noun*
A computer is an electronic machine that can **analyze** and store information. There are two kinds of computers, analog computers and **digital** computers. Most are digital. The biggest of these are called mainframes, and the smallest are called microcomputers.
He used a computer to store all the information on the forestry program.

concentric   *adjective*
Concentric describes things that have the same center. A group of **circles** that share the same center are called concentric circles.
When the pebble was thrown into the pond, the ripples formed concentric circles.

cone   *noun*
A cone is a kind of **solid shape** or **polyhedron**. It has a flat **circular** bottom and sloping sides. The sides rise up from the **base** and meet at a **point** at the top, called the **vertex**. If a cone is laid on its side, it will roll around in a **circle**.
The nose of a rocket is shaped like a cone.
conic   *adjective*

congruent   *adjective*
In **geometry**, congruent describes things that are exactly the same **size** and **shape**.
When two congruent triangles are placed on top of each other, they cover each other exactly.

31

constant   adjective
Constant describes things that do not change. Something that is constant can be used to **measure** how much other things change. A **ruler** is a constant **length**, so it can be used to measure the length of other objects. The opposite of constant is **variable**.
The temperature at which water freezes is constant.

construct   verb
In **geometry**, to construct is to make a careful, accurate drawing. It is usually done by following mathematical instructions and using special equipment.
She was asked to construct a nautilus using a ruler and a compass.
construction   noun

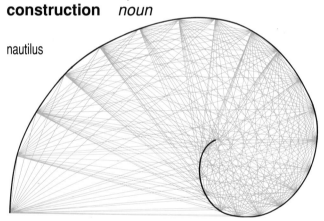

nautilus

consumer   noun
A consumer is a person who **buys** things for his or her own use.
There are laws to protect consumers from being cheated.

consumer price index   noun
The consumer price index is a **measure** of the cost of living. It is based on changes in **retail prices**. Usually it is **computed** from the prices of a selection of **goods** and **services**. Every so often new prices are compared to those given when the survey started. This shows how much prices have gone up or down.
The consumer price index showed that prices in the country were gradually dropping.

contract   noun
A contract is a legal agreement between two or more people or **organizations**. Each agrees to do something for the other. Very often, the agreement is that one party will provide **goods** or **services** in exchange for **payment** by the other party.
She entered into a contract to rent the apartment for two years.

conversion ► page 33

convert   verb
To convert is to change from one **measure** to another. The **currency** of one country can be converted into the currency of another.
At the bureau de change, she converted her American dollars into British pounds.

coordinates   plural noun
Coordinates are **numbers** or letters that indicate a position on a **graph** or a **map**. The coordinates of each **point** on a graph are shown on the **axes** of the graph. When we map out Earth's **surface** we use **lines** of **longitude** and **latitude** to make coordinates.
She used coordinates on her map to find the location of the city.

córdoba   noun
The córdoba is the **currency** of Nicaragua. It is made up of 100 centavos.

corporation   noun
A corporation is a group of people who are given certain legal rights that enable them to act as a single person. Corporations can **buy** and **sell property**, sign **contracts**, and **produce goods** and **services**.
The corporation bought a new truck.

corresponding angles   plural noun
Corresponding angles are pairs of **angles** made when two **lines** are crossed by another straight line. Each angle in the pair is in the same position.
The side road crossed both main roads, making corresponding angles.

conversion *noun*

Conversion is a way of changing a **measurement** into an equivalent measurement in a different system, for example, from metric to imperial.

length and distance

to convert	multiply by
inches to centimeters	2.540
centimeters to inches	0.394
feet to meters	0.305
meters to feet	3.281
yards to meters	0.914
meters to yards	1.094
miles to kilometers	1.609
kilometers to miles	0.621

surface and area

to convert	multiply by
square inches to square centimeters	6.452
square centimeters to square inches	0.155
square meters to square feet	10.764
square feet to square meters	0.093
square yards to square meters	0.836
square meters to square yards	1.196
square miles to square kilometers	2.589
square kilometers to square miles	0.386
acres to hectares	0.405
hectares to acres	2.471

temperature

To convert Celsius to Fahrenheit multiply by 9, divide by 5, and add 32.

To convert Fahrenheit to Celsius subtract 32, multiply by 5, and divide by 9.

volume

to convert	multiply by
cubic inches to cubic centimeters	16.387
cubic centimeters to cubic inches	0.061
cubic feet to cubic meters	0.028
cubic meters to cubic feet	35.314
cubic yards to cubic meters	0.765
cubic meters to cubic yards	1.308

liquid volume

to convert	multiply by
cubic inches to liters	0.164
liters to cubic inches	61.027
fluid ounces to milliliters	30.0
milliliters to fluid ounces	0.034
pints (imperial) to liters	0.568
liters to pints (imperial)	1.76
pints (American) to liters	0.47
liters to pints (American)	2.1
gallons (imperial) to liters	4.545
liters to gallons (imperial)	0.22
gallons (American) to liters	3.8
liters to gallons (American)	0.26

weight and mass

to convert	multiply by
grains to grams	0.065
grams to grains	15.43
ounces to grams	28.35
grams to ounces	0.035
pounds to grams	453.592
grams to pounds	0.002
pounds to kilograms	0.454
kilograms to pounds	2.205
tons to kilograms	1016.05
kilograms to tons	0.001
metric ton to short ton	1.1
short ton to metric ton	0.9

The figures in this table have been rounded to three decimal points.

cosine *noun*
The cosine is a law in **trigonometry**. It allows the **length** of one side of a **triangle** to be **calculated**, if you know the length of two sides and the size of the angle between them. For a triangle ABC, with sides a, b, and c, the law of cosine is written $C^2 = a^2 + b^2 - 2ab\,(\cos C)$.
She calculated the length of one side of the triangular shape using the cosine.

cost ▶ price

counterclockwise *adjective*
Counterclockwise describes a movement in the opposite direction to the movement of the hands on a **clock** face.
To open the door the key had to turn in a counterclockwise direction.

counterfeit *adjective*
Counterfeit describes something that is **forged**, or fake. Counterfeit **money** is printed to look like real **bank notes**.
The counterfeit money was worthless.

counting *noun*
Counting is a method of finding out how many of a certain item there are. Counting is done by using **numerals**, or **digits**, usually on a **base** of 10.
Counting the cans of fruit took the storekeeper a long time.
count *verb*

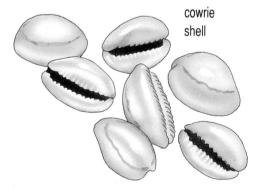
cowrie shell

cowrie shell *noun*
Cowrie shells are a type of seashell that was used as **currency** in Africa and Asia.

crash *noun*
A crash is a sudden failure of a **company** or a sudden, severe drop in the **stock market**.
After the crash of the airline company, the investors lost all their money.

credit *noun*
1. In **bookkeeping**, a credit is a kind of entry in an **account**. Credit refers to a **profit** or an item of **income earned** by a **business**.
He made a credit entry in the sales account to show the value of the sale.
2. Credit is an arrangement a **customer** can make to **pay** for **goods** or **services** sometime after he or she has bought them. The opposite of credit is immediate **payment** in **cash**.
Most businesses trade with each other on credit.

credit bureau *noun*
A credit bureau is a **company** that collects information on individuals' credit ratings. When someone applies for a **loan**, the **bank** checks with the credit bureau to see if the person is credit worthy.
The credit bureau gave her its highest rating.

credit card *noun*
A credit card is a small plastic card that can be used to **buy goods**. The **bank** that **issues** the credit card **pays** the **store** the amount of **money** the cardholder has **spent**. Then the cardholder is **billed** by the bank, usually once per **month**. If the cardholder doesn't pay his or her **balance** in full, he or she is **charged interest** for the **loan**.
She used her credit card to buy the book.

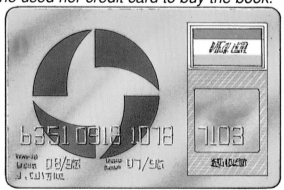

creditor *noun*
A creditor is someone to whom **money** is owed.
The company paid its creditors at the end of each month.

cross section *noun*
A cross section is the **shape** made when an object is cut through the middle. Cross sections are used to view the inside of an object.
The cross section diagram of the motor showed how it worked.

cruzado *noun*
The cruzado is the **currency** of Brazil. It is **divided** into 1,000 old cruzeiros.

cube *noun*
1. A cube is a **solid shape**, or **polyhedron**, with six faces. All the faces are **squares** of the same **size**.
She put a cube of sugar in her coffee.

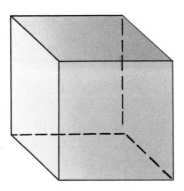

2. The cube of a **number** is the number **multiplied** by itself twice. The cube of 4 is 4 × 4 × 4 = 64. The cube of 4 is written 4^3.
The cube of 3 is 27.
cubic *adjective*

cube root *noun*
A cube root is a **number** that makes a **cube**. The cube root of 64 is 4, because the cube of 4 is 4 × 4 × 4 = 64.
She discovered that the cube root of 125 is 5.

cubic measure *noun*
Cubic measure is a **measure** of **volume** in **cubic units**.
Cubic measure was used to determine how much water was needed to fill the swimming pool.

cubit *noun*
A cubit was a **unit** of **length** used in ancient times. A cubit was the length of a person's arm from the elbow to the tip of the fingers. It **measured** about 18 to 22 **inches**.
The carpenter sawed off a piece of wood 2 cubits long.

cuboid *noun*
A cuboid is a **solid shape**, or **polyhedron**, with six faces. Each face of a cuboid is a **rectangle**. A **cube** is a special sort of cuboid that has **square** faces.
All the bricks were cuboids so they fit together easily.

currency *noun*
Currency is **money**. A currency can also mean the name of the money used in a particular country. In the United States the currency is the U.S. **dollar**, while in Britain the currency is the **pound sterling**.
The currency of Spain is the peseta.

current asset *noun*
A current asset is an **asset** that is either **money** already, or one that can be changed into money fairly quickly. Money in a **bank account** is a current asset. The **inventory** in a **store** is also a current asset, because **customers** will eventually **buy** it for **cash**.
The company's current assets included cash and inventory.

curve *noun*
A curve is a **line** that bends smoothly. It has no straight parts or sharp corners.
The player kicked the ball in a curve towards the goal.
curved *adjective*

customs   *plural noun*

Customs are a kind of **duty**, or tax, paid on goods imported into a country. Each country has its own rules about what goods are allowed to be imported, and how much duty is payable. At a port or airport, passengers and their luggage are checked by customs inspectors. In many countries some items, such as illegal drugs and weapons, may be confiscated.

The customs officer asked him to open his suitcase.

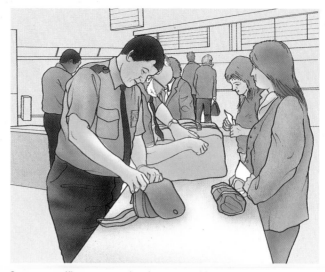

Customs officers may check personal luggage.

Customs boats patrol the harbor, ready to solve any problems.

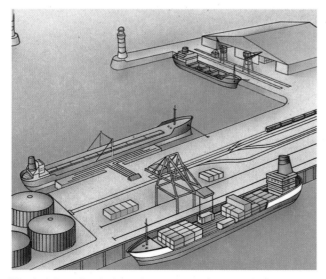

The freight unloaded at a busy port needs special documentation.

Customs officers may make a thorough search if they suspect a traveler of importing something illegally.

Shipments of food must be carefully checked. Many countries don't allow certain products through in an effort to try and stop the spread of pests or diseases.

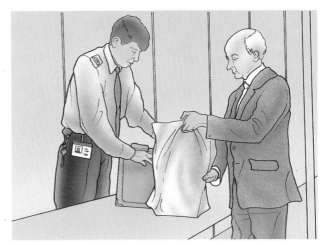

Passengers are usually allowed a certain number of duty-free goods.

Items made of ivory, crocodile skin, and other rare materials can not be brought in to many countries without special permission.

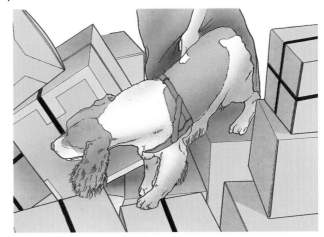

Trained dogs are used to detect hidden drugs.

customer   *noun*
A customer is someone who **buys** something.
The customer bought a loaf of bread.

customs ► page 36

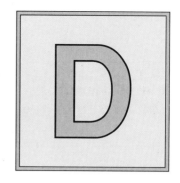

Danish krone   (plural **kroner**) *noun*
The Danish krone is the **currency** of Denmark. The krone is made up of 100 öre.

data   (singular **datum**)   *plural noun*
Data means information or facts. In **finance** the word data is often used to indicate information that is put into or stored in a **computer** by **accountants**. Data can also be **withdrawn**, or output, from a computer to allow an **analysis**.
All the data on the financial results were sent to the accountant.

day   *noun*
A day is the **time** it takes for Earth to turn once on its **axis** as it spins around the sun. We count this time as 24 **hours**. Astronomers **measure** the **length** of a day more accurately as 23 hours, 56 **minutes**. We sometimes use the term day to describe the hours of daylight and night for the period of darkness.
They went on vacation for four days.

deadbeat   *noun*
Deadbeat is a slang term for a person who tries to get out of paying debts.
She called him a deadbeat because he still hasn't paid her back.

deal   *noun*
A deal is an agreement. It is made when one person agrees to do **business** with another. A deal usually involves **buying** or **selling** **goods** or **services**.
He made a good deal when he bought the car for only $1,000.

dealer ► trader

debit *noun*
In **bookkeeping**, a debit is a type of entry in an **account**. A debit is a **loss** or an **expense** made by a **business**. The opposite of debit is **credit**.
He made a debit entry of $4,000 to show the cost of the new machine.

debt *noun*
A debt is an amount of **money** that is owed to someone.
His debt of $400 had to be repaid to the bank before January.

debtor *noun*
A debtor is someone who owes **money**.
The company asked all its debtors to pay their bills.

decade *noun*
A decade is a span of **time** lasting 10 **years**. Ten decades make a **century**.
Parts of Africa have suffered a severe drought for the past decade.

decagon *noun*
A decagon is a flat **shape** with 10 sides. In a **regular** decagon, all the sides are the same **length**. The **interior angles** of a regular decagon each **measure** 144°. An irregular decagon can be any shape.
She drew a decagon with a ruler and compass, carefully measuring each angle.

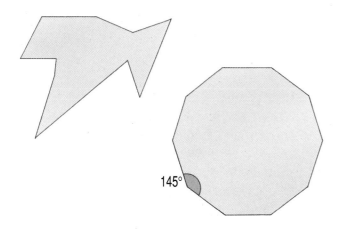

145°

decimal *adjective*
Decimal describes **counting** in tens. Decimal counting uses **base** 10. In decimal counting, 1,835 means 1 thousand, 8 hundreds, 3 tens and 5 **units**. A decimal **currency** is based on multiples and fractions of 10.
The decimal system began when the earliest people used their fingers to count.
decimalization *verb*

decrease *verb*
To decrease is to get smaller. In **mathematics**, totals decrease as **lesser numbers** are **subtracted** from them.
The amount of money in her bank decreased after she paid her bills at the end of the month.

deduct *verb*
To deduct is to take away or **subtract**.
When you deduct 9 from 31, you are left with 22.
deduction *noun*

deficit *noun*
A deficit is a lack of **money** that occurs when the amount **spent** is greater than the amount **received**. In **accounting** terms, this means that **expenditure** is greater than **income**. Individuals, **companies**, and even countries can all experience deficits at times. The opposite of deficit is **surplus**.
The company's accounts showed a deficit of $100,000 for the year.

deflation *noun*
Deflation is a reduction in the amount of **money** available to spend, which makes **prices** fall. It usually occurs when people, **companies**, or countries cut back on how much money they spend. During periods of deflation, there is less activity in the **economy**.
In times of deflation, prices generally go down.
deflate *verb*
deflationary *adjective*

degree *noun*
1. A degree is a **measurement** of an arc or an **angle**. Degrees can be measured with a **protractor**. A right angle measures 90 degrees. One full **rotation** measures 360 degrees. The **symbol** for degree is °.
The balloon drifted several degrees off course.
2. A degree is a **unit** of **measurement** for temperature. Water freezes at 32 degrees Fahrenheit and boils at 212 degrees Fahrenheit, or 100 degrees Celsius.
The temperature on Thursday was 70 degrees Fahrenheit.

demand *noun*
Demand is something **customers** want to **buy**, as well as how much of it they require.
The store bought extra candy to meet the sudden demand from its customers.

denarius *noun*
The denarius was a **silver coin** used in ancient Rome. The coin was first **issued** about 211 B.C.
A denarius was often stamped with the head of the emperor.

denary *adjective*
Denary means having to do with the **number** 10. The denary system, in which **units** are sorted into groups of ten, is more often called the **decimal** system, or **base** 10.
In the denary system you count in hundreds, tens, and units.

denomination *noun*
A denomination is the **value** printed on a **coin** or **bank note**, or its **face value**.
The denominations of the coins in his pocket were 10 cents and 25 cents.

denominator *noun*
The denominator of a **fraction** is the **number** written below the line. The denominator shows how many parts a whole number has been split, or **divided**, into. It is the number that is being divided into the top number.
The denominator of the fraction $\frac{4}{7}$ is 7.

deposit *verb*
To deposit is to put **money** into a **bank account**. The opposite of deposit is **withdraw**.
He deposited the check in his bank account at the end of the month.

deposit *noun*
A deposit is an amount of **money paid** in advance to a **supplier**. If a **customer** wants to **buy** a washing machine that must be specially ordered, the **store** may ask the customer to **pay** part of the **price** as a deposit.
A deposit helps to make sure that a customer completes a deal.

depreciate *verb*
To depreciate is to fall in **value**. **Goods** normally depreciate in value as they are used or become older.
The value of the car will depreciate over the coming year.
depreciation *noun*

depression *noun*
A depression is a period when the **economy** is not very active. During a depression, many people become **unemployed**, **factories** make fewer **products**, and people **buy** fewer **goods**.
Even for people who still have a job, wages can fall during a depression.

design ▶ **pattern**

deutsche mark *noun*
The deutsche mark, sometimes spelled deutschmark, is the **currency** of Germany. The deutsche mark is made up of 100 pfennigs.

devalue *verb*
To devalue is to make something worth **less** than it used to be.
The government decided to devalue its currency compared to other currencies.
devaluation *noun*

diagonal *noun*
A diagonal is a **straight line** that can be drawn across a **shape** from one corner to another. If you draw a diagonal across a **square** you will cut the square into two equal **triangles**.
She cut the silk square along the diagonal to make two head scarves.

diagram *noun*
A diagram is a drawing used to illustrate a **problem** in **geometry**. It can also be a plan or a **chart** that shows a simple outline of a more difficult **construction**.
He drew a diagram to show how far the planets are from the sun.

diameter *noun*
The diameter of a **circle** is the **distance** from one side to the other through its center **point**. This distance is always twice the **length** of the **radius**.
The diameter of the giant waterlily leaf was more than four feet.

diamond ▶ **rhombus**

die (plural **dice**) *noun*
A die is a small **polyhedron**, usually with a group of dots or a **number** stamped on each of its faces. When the die is a **cube**, the number of dots generally stands for the numbers 1, 2, 3, 4, 5, and 6.
A die is thrown in many board games to decide how many spaces a player can move.

difference *noun*
The difference between two **numbers** is the answer you get when one number is **subtracted** from the other.
The difference between 7 and 3 is 4.

digit *noun*
A digit is a single **number**. In the **decimal** system of **counting**, the digits are 0, 1, 2, 3, 4, 5, 6, 7, 8, 9. Digits can be used to write larger numbers. The number 7,428 has four digits, 7, 4, 2, and 8. In the **binary** system, there are only two digits, 0 and 1. Another name for a digit is a **numeral**.
The smallest digit in the number 7835 is 3.

digital *adjective*
Digital describes anything that uses **digits** to display information.
My digital telephone number is 723-4660.

dime *noun*
A dime is a **coin** used in the United States and Canada. It is worth ten **cents**.

dimension ▶ page 42

dimension   *noun*

Dimension is a **measurement**, such as length or thickness. A straight piece of thread has one dimension, that of length. A flat piece of paper has two dimensions, its length and its width. A box has three dimensions, length, width and height.

The dimensions of the backyard are 100 feet wide and 100 feet long.

This boat has been drawn to show two dimensions, length and height.

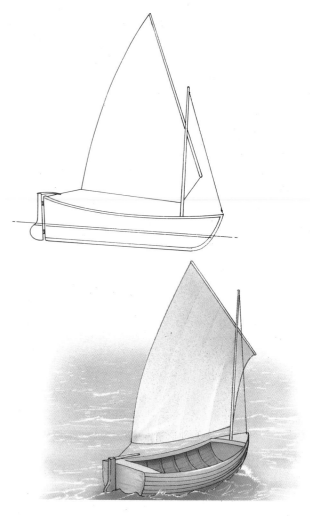

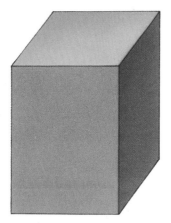

A square has two dimensions, length and height.

A cube has three dimensions, length, width, and height.

Artists use perspective to create an impression of depth. In this drawing the boat appears to have three dimensions.

Artists can play with perspective to create shapes on paper that couldn't really exist as objects.

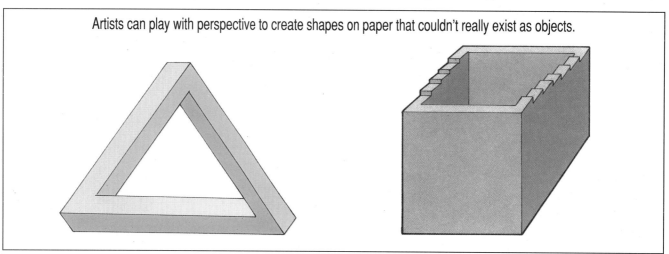

42

dinar *noun*
The dinar is the unit of **currency** in several countries, such as Algeria, Jordan, and Tunisia. In Algeria, one dinar is worth 100 centimes. In Jordan one dinar is divided into 1,000 fils, and in Tunisia into 1,000 millimes.

directed number *noun*
A directed number is a **number** that has a plus or minus sign before it. A plus number is a **positive number**; a minus number is a **negative number**.
Negative numbers are directed numbers.

director *noun*
A director is a person who manages the **business** of a **company**. A company usually has several directors, who together make up the **board of directors**. The directors are chosen by the people who own the company, the **shareholders**.
The directors decided that the company should begin to make a new product.

direct proportion *noun*
Direct proportion means that one **measurement** changes at the same **rate** as another. For example, if two **pounds** of fruit cost $3, then four pounds will cost $6. The weight of the fruit and the **cost** of the fruit change in direct proportion.
The wall grew taller in direct proportion to the number of bricks used.
proportional *adjective*

dirham *noun*
The dirham is the unit of **currency** in Morocco and in the United Arab Emirates. In Morocco one dirham is equal in value to 100 centimes. In the United Arab Emirates one dirham is made up of 100 fils.

discount *noun*
A discount is a **reduction** in **price**. **Goods** are normally sold at a discount to encourage people to **buy** them.
The full price of the book was $20 but with the discount it was only $17.

distance *noun*
Distance is the **measurement** between two places or **points**. The **metric units** of distance or **length**, are **kilometers**, **meters**, **centimeters**, and **millimeters**. In **imperial measurements**, distance is **calculated** in **miles**, **yards**, **feet**, and **inches**.
She measured the distance between the two trees as 19 feet.

distributive *adjective*
Distributive describes an operation in multiplication in which each term in a **number** or **equation** can be multiplied separately by the multiplier without changing the result. For example, $3 \times (3 + 2) = 15$, and $(3 \times 3) + (3 \times 2) = 15$.
The distributive law can be used only in multiplication.

dividend *noun*
A dividend is **money paid** by a **company** to its **shareholders**.
Dividends are often paid yearly.

divisibility test ► page 44

division *noun*
Division is a kind of **arithmetic**. The **symbol** for division is ÷. If there are twelve biscuits and six people to share them then division is used to work out that each person can have two biscuits. $12 \div 6 = 2$.
We use division to divide things equally.
divide *verb*

dodecagon *noun*
A dodecagon is a twelve-sided flat, or plane, **shape**. It is a **polygon**.
The sides of a regular dodecagon are equal.

dodecahedron *noun*
A dodecahedron is a **solid shape**, or **polyhedron**, with twelve faces.
The twelve faces of a dodecahedron have five equal sides.

dollar ► page 45

divisibility test   *noun*

A divisibility test is used to find out whether or not one number is divisible, or can be divided equally, by another number. For instance, a number is divisible by 2 if it ends in 0, 2, 4, 6 or 8. If you apply the divisibility test to the number 146 you can see that it ends in 6, so it must be divisible by 2.

We practiced using divisibility tests in class today.

A number is divisible:

by 2 if it ends in 0, 2, 4, 6, or 8

by 4 if its last two digits are divisible by 4

16 will divide exactly by 4 so the whole number 2,716 is divisible by 4

$2,716 \div 4 = 679$

by 3 if its digits add up to 3, 6, or 9

$31,245 = 3 + 1 + 2 + 4 + 5 = 15 = 1 + 5 = 6$

so 31,245 is divisible by 3

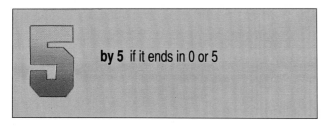

by 5 if it ends in 0 or 5

by 6 if it is an even number and divisible by 3

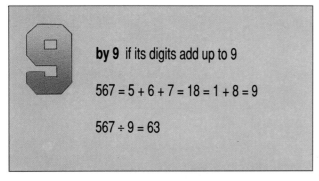

by 9 if its digits add up to 9

$567 = 5 + 6 + 7 = 18 = 1 + 8 = 9$

$567 \div 9 = 63$

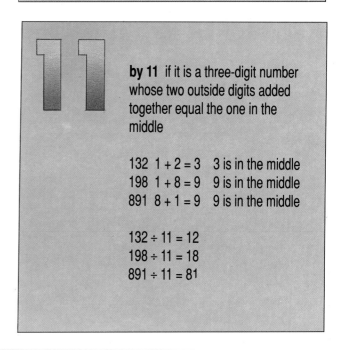

by 11 if it is a three-digit number whose two outside digits added together equal the one in the middle

132 $1 + 2 = 3$ 3 is in the middle
198 $1 + 8 = 9$ 9 is in the middle
891 $8 + 1 = 9$ 9 is in the middle

$132 \div 11 = 12$
$198 \div 11 = 18$
$891 \div 11 = 81$

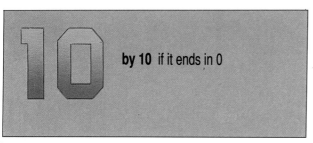

by 10 if it ends in 0

dollar noun

The dollar is the unit of currency of many countries of the world, including Australia, the Bahamas, Barbados, Belize, Canada, Dominica, Fiji, Guyana, Hong Kong, Jamaica, Liberia, New Zealand, Singapore, Taiwan, Trinidad and Tobago, the United States, and Zimbabwe. The word came from the English for the German 'thaler'. The sign for dollar is $.

Many countries issue their dollar in both paper notes and coins.

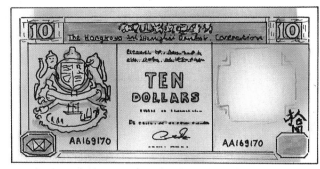

Hong Kong dollar notes of $10 and over are issued by the Hong Kong and Shanghai Banking Corporation and the Standard Chartered Bank.

The American dollar became the official currency of the United States in 1792. It is issued as $1, $2, $5, $10, $20, $50, and $100 notes.

The Singapore $20 note features a yellow-breasted sunbird.

The Canadian dollar is circulated as a $1 coin, and $1, $2, $5, $10, $20, $50, $100 and $1,000 paper notes.

The Singapore dollar is issued as a $1 coin and $1, $5, $10, $20, $50, $100, $1,000 and $10,000 paper notes.

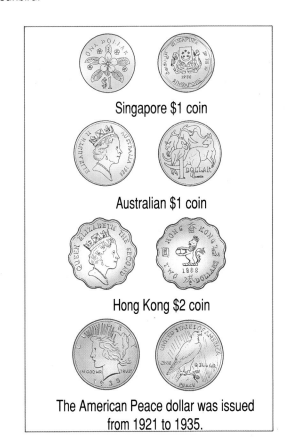

Singapore $1 coin

Australian $1 coin

Hong Kong $2 coin

The American Peace dollar was issued from 1921 to 1935.

double *verb*
To double is to **multiply** by 2.
After taking a rest, he set off at double his previous speed.

doubloon *noun*
A doubloon was a **gold coin** used in Spain until the 1800s.
In olden days, pirates raided Spanish merchant ships to steal their treasure of doubloons.

Dow Jones Index *noun*
The Dow Jones Index is an **index**, or **number**, that indicates the **value** of **stocks** on the New York Stock Exchange, compared to past levels. It changes continually as stocks are **bought** and **sold**.
The Dow Jones Index rose on Tuesday as more people bought shares.

dozen *noun*
A dozen is another word for 12.
The chef beat together a dozen eggs to make the omelets.

drachma *noun*
The drachma is the **currency** of Greece. One drachma is worth 100 lepta.

draft *noun*
Draft is another word for **check**. It is a written order for a **bank** or other institution to **pay money** from one **account** to another.
He paid for the boat with a bank draft.

ducat *noun*
Ducat was the name given to several different kinds of **gold** or **silver coins** that were once used in Europe.

duodecimal *adjective*
A duodecimal system is a number system in which the **base** is 12. In base 12, the number 34 shows that there are four units and three 12s. There are 12 symbols in base 12; 0–9 are used plus two others to represent 10 and 11. Usually letter symbols are used such as x or y.
British currency used to use a duodecimal system before converting to the decimal system.

duty *noun*
Duty is a kind of **tax**. When **goods** are **imported**, **exported**, or **sold**, an extra amount of **money** sometimes has to be paid to the government. This extra **payment** is called the duty.
He paid duty on the jewelry he brought into the country.

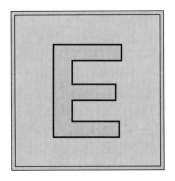

eagle *noun*
An eagle was a **gold coin** once used in the United States. It was worth $10.

earnings *plural noun*
Earnings are the amount of **money paid** to a person for doing a **job**. It is also another word for **profit**.
He spent his earnings on vacation in Greece.
earn *verb*

economics *noun*
Economics is the study of all the ways in which **goods** and **services** are **produced**, distributed, and used. It covers such subjects as the **circulation** of **money**, **imports** and **exports**, **earnings**, **employment** and **taxes**, **inflation** and **deflation**, and many other topics.
The analysis of a country's imports and exports is an important part of economics.

economist *noun*
An economist is a person who studies **economics**. Economists try to **forecast** what will happen to a country's **economy**.
The economists made a forecast of next year's rate of inflation.

economy *noun*
1. The economy of a country includes everything to do with the way it **produces** things and **sells** them. It also covers its system of **banks**, **stock exchanges**, and other **financial** institutions. One task of a government is to manage the country's economy so that the people who live there grow wealthier.
Unemployment rose because of the weak economy.
2. Economy also means trying to keep **costs** and **expenditures** as low as possible.
The company's directors insisted on strict economy in running the business.
economic *adjective*

ecu *noun*
An ecu was a **gold** or **silver coin** that was once used in France.

ECU *abbreviation*
ECU is short for European Currency Unit. It is a **currency** of the European Community. **Businesses** or individuals can **pay** for **goods** or take out **loans** in ECUs. It is stamped with 12 emblems to represent the 12 countries that are members of the European Community.
In Europe, some banks sell traveler's checks in ECUs.

Egyptian pound *noun*
The Egyptian pound is the **currency** of Egypt. An Egyptian pound is worth 100 piastres or 1,000 millièmes.

element ► member

47

ellipse   *noun*
An ellipse is a regular **oval**. It is the **shape** seen when a cone is cut off on a diagonal.
An ellipse has the shape of a flattened circle.
elliptical   *adjective*

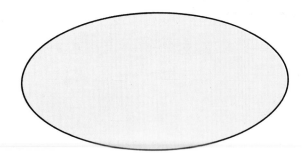

embargo   *noun*
An embargo is a ban on **importing** or **exporting goods**. For example, one country might ban the export of weapons to a country with which it is not friendly.
There is an embargo on ivory.

employee   *noun*
An employee is a person who is **paid** a **wage** or **salary** by another person, called the **employer**. Employees are paid to do a **job**, usually for a long period.
The employee was paid to deliver cheese to all the stores.
employment   *noun*

employer   *noun*
An employer is someone who **pays** a **wage** or **salary** to another person to do a **job**.
The employer needed another store clerk.
employ   *verb*

empty set   *noun*
An empty set is a **set** that has no **members**, or elements, in it. The **symbol** to show an empty set is { } or ∅.
In a boys' school, the set of girl pupils would be an empty set.

entrepreneur   *noun*
An entrepreneur is a **business** person who takes a **risk** in order to make a **profit**.
The entrepreneur started her own company.

equal   *adjective*
Equal means the same in quantity, value, size or degree. Two things that balance are equal. The equal sign, =, is used between two sides of an **equation** to show that each quantity is equal to the other.
One dollar is equal to 100 cents.

equation   *noun*
An equation is a **statement** that two things are equal. An equation is made up of two **quantities** with an equal sign (=) between them. For example, $7 = 5 + 2$ shows that the **sum** of 5 and 2 is equal to 7.
Equations are used often in algebra.

equilateral triangle   *noun*
An equilateral triangle is a **triangle** whose sides are all the same **length**. The **interior angles** of an equilateral triangle are all 60°.
Equilateral triangles can be used in tessellation.

equity   *noun*
Equity is a **share** in a particular **business** or in an **asset**. Each owner of a business will hold some equity in it. Equity is **measured** by the **number** of shares a **shareholder** owns.
He lost some of his equity in the business when he sold some of his shares.

escudo   *noun*
The escudo is the **currency** of Portugal. An escudo is worth 100 centavos. A thousand escudos is called a conto.

estimate *noun*
An estimate is a guess at the **size** of something. An estimate often is a little larger or a little smaller than the actual amount. A builder who is going to build a house will not know exactly how many bricks will be needed, but will need to estimate a quantity so that work can start.
The driver estimated he would take 2 hours.
estimate *verb*

eurodollar *noun*
A eurodollar is a dollar held in a **bank** outside the United States, especially in a European bank.
The United States uses eurodollars to pay for things bought from foreign countries.

European Currency Unit ► ECU

even number *noun*
An even number is a **number** that can be **divided** exactly by 2. For example, 4, 6, 10, and 24 are all even numbers. A number that cannot be divided exactly by two is an **odd number**. An even number always ends in 0, 2, 4, 6, or 8.
The sum of two even numbers is always an even number.

exchange rate *noun*
The exchange rate shows how much one **currency** is worth when it is changed into another currency. The exchange rates between different currencies are changing all the time.
At the present exchange rate, he will get more than 1,000 lire for one dollar.

expenditure *noun*
An expenditure is **money** that has been spent. **Companies** need to **spend** money to **buy** the **supplies** they need. For example, a printer will buy paper and ink, and possibly a new printing machine, as part of the necessary expenditures of the **business**.
The company's expenditures rose when the new machines were ordered.

expenses *plural noun*
Expenses are amounts of **money** that a **company** or **business** person needs to **spend** to perform a **job**.
The saleswoman needed to rent a car, so the company paid her expenses.

expensive *adjective*
Expensive describes things that cost a great deal of **money** to **buy**.
The dress created by the French fashion designer was very expensive.

exponent *noun*
An exponent is a number written to the right and above another number. It shows how many times a number is multiplied by itself.
Six to the exponent three is 6^3.

exponential growth ► page 50

export *verb*
To export is to **sell goods** or **services** to **customers** in other countries. The opposite of export is **import**.
This year the company will export 1,000 tractors to Brazil.

exports *plural noun*
Exports are **goods** or **services sold** to **customers** in other countries. The opposite of exports is **imports**.
If exports increase, the wealth of the country will grow.

exponential growth   *noun*

Exponential growth, also known as geometric progression, is a rapid increase in number. The first number is multiplied by a value. The result is multiplied by the same value, and so is each result after that. The equations $2 \times 3 = 6$, $6 \times 3 = 18$, $18 \times 3 = 54$ show that {6, 18, 54} is an example of exponential growth.

Exponential growth was seen in the increase of the number of fruit flies this summer.

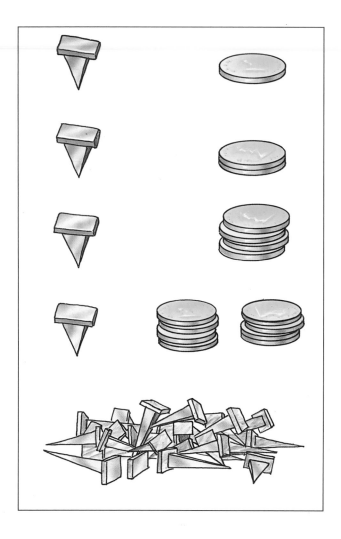

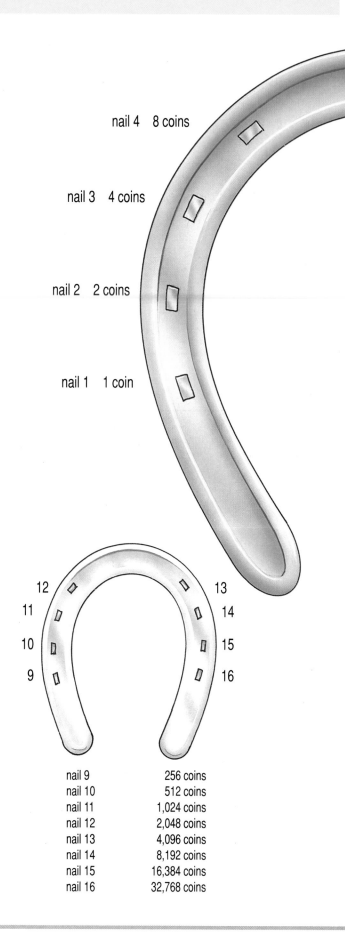

nail 4   8 coins

nail 3   4 coins

nail 2   2 coins

nail 1   1 coin

There is an old story about a blacksmith who agreed to shoe a horse for one gold coin for the first nail, two for the second, four for the third, eight for the fourth and so on. He was due 4,294,967,295 gold coins by the time the 32 nails were in place.

nail 9	256 coins
nail 10	512 coins
nail 11	1,024 coins
nail 12	2,048 coins
nail 13	4,096 coins
nail 14	8,192 coins
nail 15	16,384 coins
nail 16	32,768 coins

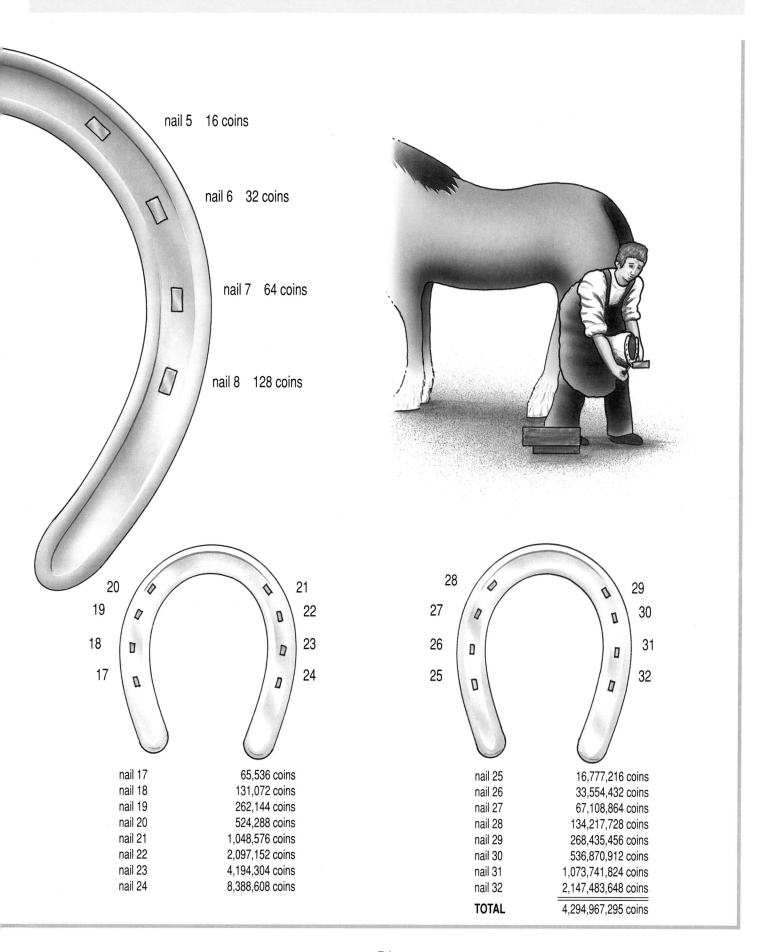

nail 5   16 coins

nail 6   32 coins

nail 7   64 coins

nail 8   128 coins

20   21
19   22
18   23
17   24

28   29
27   30
26   31
25   32

nail 17	65,536 coins
nail 18	131,072 coins
nail 19	262,144 coins
nail 20	524,288 coins
nail 21	1,048,576 coins
nail 22	2,097,152 coins
nail 23	4,194,304 coins
nail 24	8,388,608 coins

nail 25	16,777,216 coins
nail 26	33,554,432 coins
nail 27	67,108,864 coins
nail 28	134,217,728 coins
nail 29	268,435,456 coins
nail 30	536,870,912 coins
nail 31	1,073,741,824 coins
nail 32	2,147,483,648 coins
TOTAL	4,294,967,295 coins

exterior angles *plural noun*
The exterior angles of a **polygon** are the **angles** that form its **shape**. At each **point** of a polygon, the exterior angles and the **interior angles** are **supplementary angles**.
The exterior angles of a hexagon are all equal to 60°.

face value *noun*
The face value of something, such as a **bank note**, is the **value** that is printed on it. The face value of a five-**dollar** bill is five dollars. But something may be worth more than its face value. The value of a **share** of **stock** may change, so it is possible to **pay** more for it than its face value.
The broker had to pay double the face value of the shares.

factor *noun*
A factor is a **number** that **divides** equally into another number with nothing left over. Four is a factor of 12 because there are exactly three 4s in 12, so 12 can be divided by 4 exactly.
She worked out that the factors of 6 are 1, 2, 3, and 6, as each of these numbers divide equally into it.

factoring *noun*
Factoring is the process of finding all the **numbers** that are a **factor** of a particular number. The factors of 12 are 1, 2, 3, 4, 6, and 12 because 12 can be **divided** by any of these numbers.
He did the factoring of 14 and got 1, 2, 7, and 14.
factor verb

factory *noun*
A factory is a building where a **company** makes the **products** that it will sell. The factory houses the production equipment and the employees who work there.
The cars were made on an assembly line in a large factory.

Fahrenheit *noun*
Fahrenheit is a **scale** used to **measure** temperature in **degrees**. The **freezing point** of water is a **constant** 32 degrees (32°) on the Fahrenheit scale. The **boiling point** of water is 212 degrees Fahrenheit (212°). In most parts of the world, the **Celsius** scale is more widely used.
The midday temperature was 40 degrees Fahrenheit.

fare *noun*
A fare is a **payment** you make to travel on a vehicle, such as a bus, train, or plane.
He paid for his fare with some coins.

farthing *noun*
A farthing is a **coin** that was once used in Britain. It was worth a quarter of a **penny**.

Federal Reserve ► **reserve**

fee *noun*
A fee is an amount **charged** by a person who performs a **service**. **Accountants**, lawyers, and service **businesses** charge fees to their **clients**.
The company paid a fee to a consultant for advice on which computer to buy.

figure *noun*
1. A figure is a **symbol** for a **number**. Figures used in the **decimal** system of counting are made up of the **digits** 0, 1, 2, 3, 4, 5, 6, 7, 8 and 9.
The number 2,386 is a figure.
2. Figure is another word for **shape**. Figures can be **planes** or **solids**.
A circle is a plane figure, and a sphere is a solid figure.
figure *verb*

finance *noun*
Finance is the **money** used by a **business** in its day-to-day work. The term can also be used to refer to the science of managing money.
The company was seeking finance for a building project.
financial *adjective*

finance *verb*
To finance is to provide the **money** needed to create or to expand a **business**. A government will sometimes help to finance projects in regions where unemployment is high.
The investor financed the building of a new skyscraper.

Financial Times Index *noun*
The Financial Times Index is an **index**, or **number**, that indicates the present level of the **price** of **shares** at the London Stock Exchange, compared with past levels. It is based on the share prices of 30 leading British industries.
The Financial Times Index dropped as share prices went down and people sold their shares quickly.

financier *noun*
A financier is a person who **invests** large amounts of **money** in **business** ventures in the hope of making a **profit**. The investments can be made in new or existing companies.
The financier provided $1 million for the new project.

firm *noun*
A firm is a type of **business** that is not recognized as separate from its owners. A group of lawyers may form a firm, for example. A firm is different from a **corporation**.
There were seven partners in the firm of accountants.

fiscal *adjective*
Fiscal describes government activities having to do with **spending** and **taxes**. Fiscal also sometimes means having to do with **money** in a general way.
The government is planning new fiscal policies that will increase taxes.

fixed asset *noun*
A fixed asset is an **asset** that a **business** owns over a long period and that it uses to **earn profits**. A delivery van is a fixed asset because it may last for several **years** before it is replaced. An office building and a **factory** are also fixed assets since they may have a very long life.
The company's fixed assets include a printing press.

florin *noun*
1. A florin was a **gold coin** used in Florence in the thirteenth **century**.
2. Florin was the name of various coins once used in several European countries and in South Africa.

flowchart ► page 56

foot (plural **feet**) *noun*
A foot is an **imperial measure** of **length** which is equal to approximately 30 **centimeters** in the **metric system**. There are three feet in a **yard** and 5,280 feet in a **mile**.
The living room in the old house measured 17 feet by 20 feet.

forecast *verb*
To forecast is to predict what will happen in the future. In **business**, **companies** forecast how much they will **earn** in the coming **year**. They do this by **estimating** how much they will **sell** to **customers** and how high their **costs** will be.
They forecast that they would increase their profit next year.
forecast *noun*

foreign exchange *noun*
Foreign exchange is the **buying** and **selling** of **currencies**. Because **exchange rates** change from day to day, it is possible to buy U.S. **dollars** for one **price** on Monday and sell them for a different price on Friday. If the exchange rate has improved, a **profit** results; if the exchange rate has worsened, a **loss** results.
The company made a profit on foreign exchange this year.

forger *noun*
A forger is someone who makes **counterfeit money** or who signs someone else's name to documents, such as **checks**.
The forger printed a pile of new notes.

forgery *noun*
A forgery is something that is made to look like something else. Forgeries are often pieces of paper, such as **money** and letters, that are substituted for the real thing and used to cheat people.
The forgery was discovered, and the criminal was sent to jail.

forint *noun*
The forint is the **currency** of Hungary.
A forint is made up of 100 fillér.

formula (plural **formulas**) *noun*
In **algebra**, a formula is a quick way of writing a rule, or **equation**, using **symbols**. Many formulas are universal, like the formula for finding the **circumference** of a **circle** is $2\pi r$ ($2 \times \pi \times r$). Other formulas can be created to fit particular **problems**.
He worked out the area of the playing field using the correct formula.

Fort Knox *noun*
Fort Knox is a place in Kentucky where the United States government keeps some of its stores of **gold bullion**.
Tourists in the United States often visit famous Fort Knox.

fractal *noun*
A fractal is a complex geometric **pattern** representing a mathematical **equation**.
Fractal shapes can be generated by computer.

fraction ► page 58

franc *noun*
The franc is the unit of **currency** of several countries, such as Belgium, Cameroon, France, Niger, Senegal, and Switzerland. The franc is made up of 100 centimes.

fraud *noun*
Fraud is cheating. If the manager of a **company** falsifies the **accounts** and keeps **money** for his or her personal use, this is a case of fraud. Fraud is a crime.
He went to prison for fraud.

free trade *noun*
Free trade is **trade** across the borders of countries that is not hindered by governments. It refers to **goods** that are exchanged without **taxes** or **duty** being added.
The government allowed foreign goods to enter the country under its free trade policy.

freezing point *noun*
Freezing point is the temperature at which a liquid turns into a solid. Because the freezing point of water is a **constant**, we can use it to help **measure** temperature.
The freezing point of water is 32°F.

French franc *noun*
The French franc is the **currency** of France. It is **divided** into 100 centimes.

function *noun*
A function is the relationship of one **variable** to another. The quantity, or **value**, of one variable is related to that of the other. The acceleration of a car is a function. The variables are the car's speed and the time it started to move. If either one of those numbers change, the other is affected.
Her graph showed that price was a function of size.

fund *noun*
1. A fund is an amount of **money** set aside for a particular purpose. Money is often put into a fund in order to save for a future purchase.
The office built up a tea and coffee fund of $25.
2. Funds is a term sometimes used in a very general way to mean money.
She had enough funds to buy a new coat.

flowchart *noun*

A flowchart is a diagram that shows the steps in solving a problem. The steps are ordered in sequence, so that each must be resolved before proceeding to the next. Flowcharts are generally used as visual aids to help make complex problems easier to analyze.

He used a flowchart to show each step of the solution.

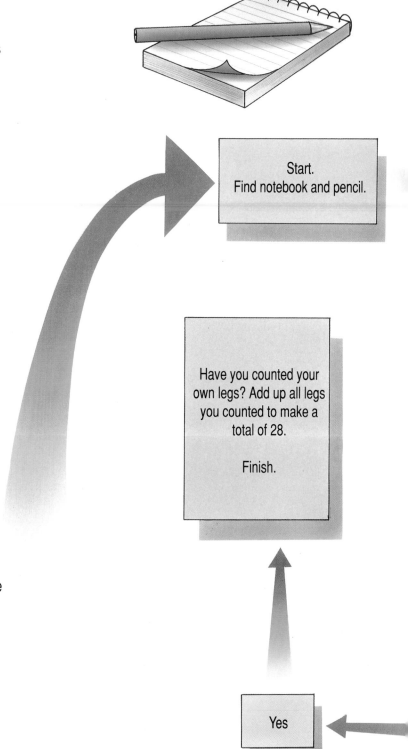

Start.
Find notebook and pencil.

Have you counted your own legs? Add up all legs you counted to make a total of 28.

Finish.

Yes

Count the legs

This flowchart shows how to count the number of legs there are in the house. The chart helps to make sure that no leg is left uncounted. As you proceed to each stage, you have to remember to write down the number of legs in each place. The flowchart reminds you to think carefully. If you made a mistake, you can return to an earlier stage and correct the mistake.

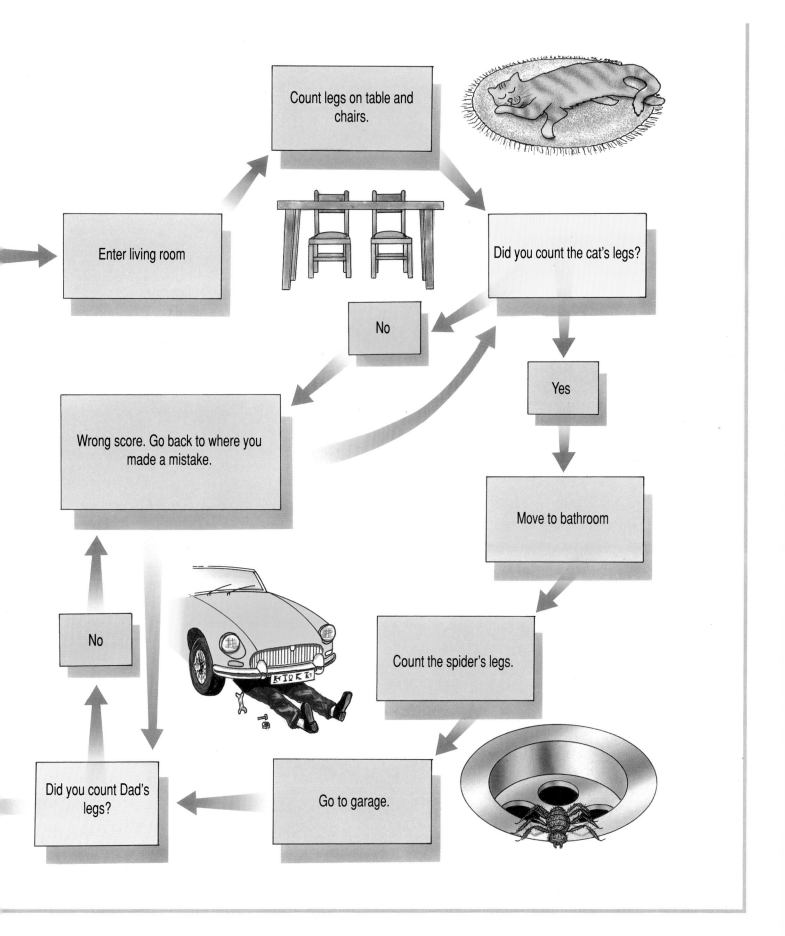

Enter living room

Count legs on table and chairs.

Did you count the cat's legs?

No

Yes

Wrong score. Go back to where you made a mistake.

Move to bathroom

Count the spider's legs.

No

Did you count Dad's legs?

Go to garage.

fraction   *noun*

A fraction is a small part of something. Fractions are usually written as two numbers separated by a line, or **bar**. The **denominator** is the number below the bar. It is the number of equal parts something has been divided into. The top number, or **numerator**, tells how many of those parts there are. Fractions can also be written, or expressed, as a **ratio**.

He divided the cake into six fractions.

Equivalent fractions can have different numerators and denominators. For example, one half can be written $\frac{6}{12}$, $\frac{5}{10}$, $\frac{4}{8}$, $\frac{2}{4}$, or $\frac{1}{2}$. When one half is written as $\frac{1}{2}$ the fraction is using the lowest common denominator.

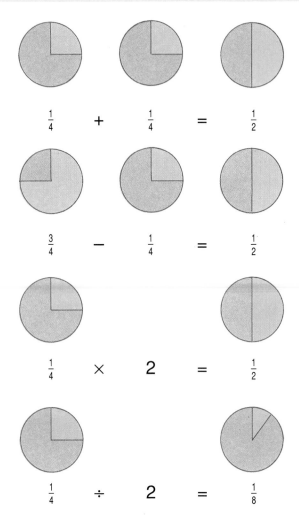

$$\frac{1}{4} + \frac{1}{4} = \frac{1}{2}$$

$$\frac{3}{4} - \frac{1}{4} = \frac{1}{2}$$

$$\frac{1}{4} \times 2 = \frac{1}{2}$$

$$\frac{1}{4} \div 2 = \frac{1}{8}$$

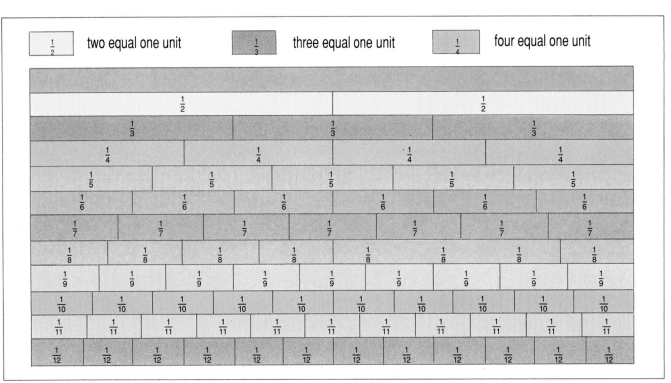

$\frac{1}{2}$ two equal one unit	$\frac{1}{3}$ three equal one unit	$\frac{1}{4}$ four equal one unit

58

fund   *verb*
To fund a project means the same as to
finance a project.
The government decided to fund a housing
project.

gain ► **profit**

gallon   *noun*
A gallon is an **imperial measure** of liquid.
It is equivalent to 4.546 liters in the **metric**
system. A gallon is **divided** into four
quarts.
The car needed 12 gallons of gasoline to fill
up the tank.

gamble   *verb*
To gamble is to take a **risk** to make **money**.
Some people gamble by playing games at a
casino or by placing **bets** on racehorses. A
company may gamble that they will **sell** a
large number of their new **products**.
At a race course, racegoers gamble on the
winning horse.

geometry   *noun*
Geometry is the study of **lines**, **shapes**, and
angles. Geometry is used to work out the
angles in a **polygon**, but **trigonometry** is
used when the polygon is a **triangle**.
The pupils drew and measured shapes in
geometry class.

gold *noun*

Gold is a rare yellow metal. For thousands of years, people have valued gold because it is not affected by air or water, so it never rusts or grows dull. It is also soft, and easy to work into different shapes. Gold was once used to make coins, but is now used mainly in jewelry and in industry.

She bought a necklace made of gold.

Lumps of gold called nuggets are sometimes found.

Gold may be dug from mines underground.

Some grains of gold are found in the bed of a river. The gold is separated from the mud and gravel by panning.

Gold is also obtained from open mines.

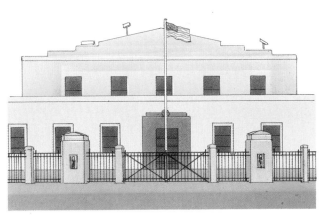

Much of the gold owned by the government of the United States is kept at Fort Knox, Kentucky.

Some countries hold large reserves of gold bullion.

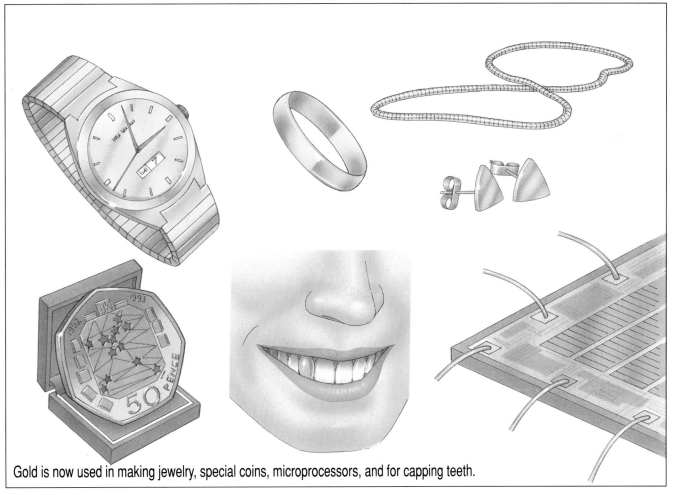

Gold is now used in making jewelry, special coins, microprocessors, and for capping teeth.

gift certificate　noun
A gift certificate is a printed form showing a certain amount of **money**; it can be bought from a **store** and given to someone, who can then use it to make purchases at the store.
For his birthday, he received a $25 gift certificate.

gilt-edged security　*noun*
A gilt-edged security is an investment in a **company** with a very sound financial record.
His investment portfolio contained nothing but gilt-edged securities.

gold ► page 60

golden ratio ► ratio

goldsmith　*noun*
A goldsmith is a person who makes objects out of **gold**.
The goldsmith made a gold ring.

gold standard　*noun*
The gold standard was a system used in the past to fix the **value** of a **currency**. For example, if a **coin** or **note** was given a value equal to the **price** of an **ounce** of gold, the value of that currency would change whenever the value of gold changed.
The gold standard is no longer in use since it caused many difficulties.

goods　*plural noun*
Goods are **products** that can be **bought**. Food, clothes, books, furniture, and electronics are all examples of goods that can be bought in **stores**.
The store ordered more goods.

gradient ► slope

gram　*noun*
A gram is a **metric unit** of **weight**. A gram is equal to $\frac{1}{28}$ of an **ounce**.
Scientists often measure substances in grams.

graph ► page 63

greenback　*noun*
Greenback is a term that sometimes refers to the paper money used in the USA.
She spent her last greenback on chocolate.

grid　noun
A grid is a crisscross **diagram** of **straight lines**. **Graphs** are often recorded on a grid, and a grid is used to form **coordinates** on a **map**.
He charted the team's scores on a grid.

gross　*noun*
Gross means complete, or with nothing taken out. It can refer to **wages earned** before any **taxes**, or to **profit** that a **company** makes before it **deducts expenses**. A gross is also 12 **dozen** (144) of something.
The company had a gross profit of $1 million.

Gross National Product　*noun*
Gross National Product is the total **value** in money of all the **goods** and **services** produced by a country during a particular period, plus the net income it receives from other countries. It is used to work out whether the economy of a country is improving or declining.
The Gross National Product of the country was calculated in billions of dollars.

gross profit　*noun*
Gross profit is the **money** that is **earned** from **selling goods**, **less** the money it cost to **buy** them.
The company earned a gross profit of a million dollars last year from selling lamps.

guarantee　*noun*
A guarantee is a promise that something will be repaired or replaced for free if it does not work properly. Most **products** are sold with a guarantee.
The guarantee on the refrigerator was for one year.

graph *noun*

A graph is a diagram, normally drawn on a **grid**, that shows how two or more sets of information are related. A line graph has two axes. The vertical **axis** points upward, and the horizontal axis is drawn from left to right. Another kind of graph, a bar chart, is made up of vertical or horizontal bars. A block graph compares information in blocks of different size.

A graph was drawn to show the number of refugees arriving in the camp each day.

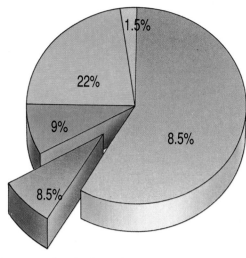

Each sector of a pie chart gives a percentage of the whole.

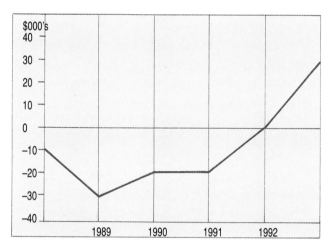

This line graph is used to show a current account balance. One axis is for years, the other for money.

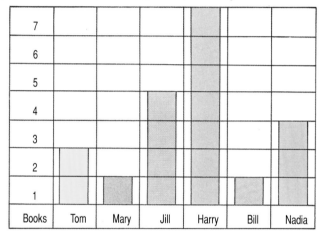

An easy-to-read bar graph shows how many books each child has read in a given space of time.

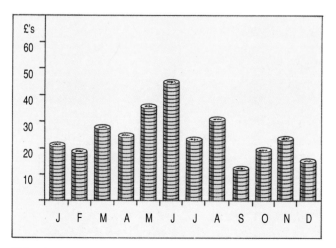

This pictograph uses pictures of money to show savings over a 12 month period.

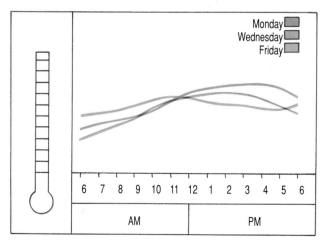

A multiple graph like this can be used to show different sets of information. Here temperature is shown for a period of three days.

guilder *noun*
The guilder is the **currency** of the
Netherlands. A guilder is made up of 100
cents.

guinea *noun*
A guinea was a **gold coin** once used in
Britain. It was worth 21 shillings, or 1.05
pounds.

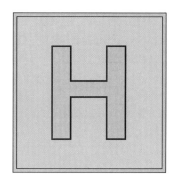

half (plural **halves**) *noun*
A half is a **fraction**. When you halve a
number or an object, you **divide** it into two
equal parts. Half of six is three because
there are two threes in six.
A semicircle is half a circle.

half dollar *noun*
A half dollar is a **coin** used in the United
States and Canada. It is worth 50¢.

heads and tails *plural noun*
Heads and tails are the faces of a **coin**. In
many countries, one side of each coin has
the head of the country's ruler on it. This
side is called heads. The other side is called
tails. Heads and tails are sometimes used to
decide who will start a sporting event. One
player chooses heads and the other player
chooses tails, and the coin is tossed to see
who wins.
*The coin showed heads, so the visiting team
kicked off.*

heads   tails

hectare *noun*
A hectare is a **unit** of **area** in the **metric
system**. It is equal to 10,000 **square meters**
or 2.471 **acres**.
*The builder bought two hectares of land for
his building site.*

height *noun*
The height of an object is the **distance** from the bottom to the top.
The height of the flagpole was 20 feet.

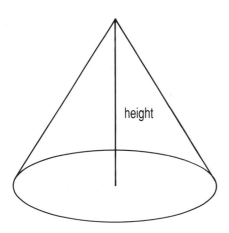

height

hemisphere *noun*
A hemisphere is a **solid shape**. If a **sphere** is cut in **half** through its center, the two halves are called hemispheres.
The dome of the Capitol building is shaped like a hemisphere.

hexagon *noun*
A hexagon is a **shape** with six straight sides and six **angles**. If all the sides and angles are equal the shape is called a **regular** hexagon.
The interior angles of a hexagon are all equal to 120°.
hexagonal *adjective*

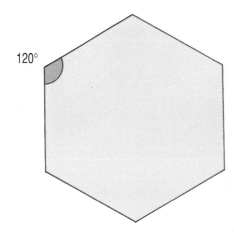

120°

hexahedron ► shape

hexamine *noun*
A hexamine is a **shape** made up of six **squares**. Hexamines are often used as the basis of **patterns**.
He laid the paving stones in the garden as a hexamine.

highest common factor *noun*
The highest common factor, or H.C.F., of two **numbers** is the largest **factor** that **divides** into both of the numbers evenly. The numbers 12 and 18 can each be broken down into factors. 12 has the factors 1, 2, 3, 4, 6, and 12, and 18 has the factors 1, 2, 3, 6, and 18. The largest factor that is in both these **sets** of factors is 6, so 6 is the highest common factor of 12 and 18.
The highest common factor of 8 and 6 is 2.

Hindu-Arabic numbers *noun*
Hindu-Arabic numbers originally came from the Hindus of India. Their number system of nine numerals was adopted by the Arabs. The Arabs introduced a tenth numeral, 'sifr', or zero.
Hindu-Arabic numerals are used throughout the Arab-speaking world today.

hire *verb*
1. Hire means to pay **money** for the use of something.
They hired a hall for the wedding.
2. Hire means to allow something to be used in exchange for **payment**.
The farmer hires out his tractor.
3. Hire means to **employ** a person to do a job.
He hired five new employees last month to work in the café.
hire *noun*

histogram ► bar chart

hoard *noun*
A hoard is an amount of **money** or valuables that has been saved.
The hoard of jewelry was found to be worth $250,000.

65

Hong Kong dollar *noun*
The Hong Kong dollar is the **currency** of Hong Kong. It is equal to 100 cents.

Hong Seng Index *noun*
The Hong Seng Index is a **number**, or **index**, that indicates the movement of **share prices** on the Hong Kong Stock Exchange. This **increases** or **decreases** in **proportion** to the movement of share prices. The Index can **vary** from minute to minute, depending on the level of share activity.
The Hong Seng Index is studied to see how share prices in Hong Kong are selling.

horizontal *adjective*
Horizontal means **parallel** to the ground. The opposite of horizontal is **vertical**.
The surface of a table is horizontal if all 4 legs are completely level.

hour *noun*
An hour is a **unit** of **time**. There are 24 **hours** in a **day**. Each hour is made up of 60 **minutes**.
The party lasted for four hours.

hourglass *noun*
An hourglass is a glass tube that measures **time**. The tube is very narrow at the middle and contains sand. It takes an **hour** for the sand to fall from the top half of the tube to the bottom.
People now use a clock instead of an hourglass.

hyperbola *noun*
A hyperbola is a kind of **curve**. If a **cone** is sliced **vertically**, the outline of the flat **shape** left behind is a hyperbola. It is called a conic section. Circles and ellipses are also conic sections.
Some comets follow a hyperbola when they travel past the Sun.
hyperbolic *adjective*

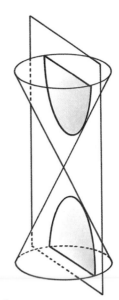

hyperinflation ► **inflation**

hypotenuse *noun*
The hypotenuse of a **right triangle** is the side that is opposite to the **right angle**. It is always the longest of the three sides. According to **Pythagorean theorem**, the **length** of the hypotenuse equals the **sum** of the **squares** of the other two sides.
She measured the hypotenuse with her ruler.

hypothesis (plural **hypotheses**) *noun*
A hypothesis is a kind of guess. For example, in an investigation about how plants grow, you might guess that their **heights** would be different in different types of soil. To test a hypothesis, an experiment must be carried out.
The hypothesis that iron is heavier than aluminium was found to be true.
hypothesize *verb*

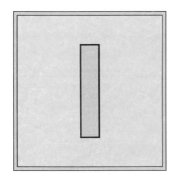

Icelandic króna (plural **krónur**)   *noun*
The Icelandic króna is the **currency** of Iceland. There are 100 aurar to the króna.

icosahedron   *noun*
An icosahedron is a **solid shape**, or **polyhedron**, that has twenty faces.
Each face of an icosahedron is a triangle.

IMF   *abbreviation*
The IMF, or International Monetary Fund, is an organization that can help countries that have trouble with their **balance of payments**. Countries that **import** many **goods** from overseas may not have enough foreign **currency** to **pay** for them all. They can sometimes **borrow** from the IMF to solve this problem.
The country asked for a loan from the IMF to fund its industrial expansion.

imperial measures   *plural noun*
Imperial measures are **standard measures** of **length**, **volume**, and **weight** formerly used in Great Britain. Many countries around the world, including the United States, adopted these measures. Today, few countries still use them. Most have adopted the **metric system** of measurement instead.
Feet, quarts and pounds are all examples of imperial measures.

import   *verb*
To import is to **buy goods** or **services** from **suppliers** in other countries. The opposite of import is **export.**
This year the company will import 1,000 tons of coffee from Brazil.

imports   *plural noun*
Imports are **goods** or **services bought** from **suppliers** in other countries. If imports are higher than exports, the **balance of payments** will suffer. The opposite of imports is **exports**.
We import electronics from Japan.

improper fraction   *noun*
An improper fraction is one in which the **numerator** is bigger than the **denominator**. An improper fraction represents a **mixed number** in **fraction** form. $\frac{13}{4}$, $\frac{26}{6}$, $\frac{7}{3}$ are all improper fractions.
She turned the improper fraction into a mixed number by dividing by the denominator.

inch   *noun*
An inch is a **unit** of **length** in the **imperial system** of **measure**. There are 12 inches in a **foot** and 36 inches in a **yard**. An inch is equal to 2.54 **centimeters**.
The disk measured $4\frac{1}{2}$ inches across.

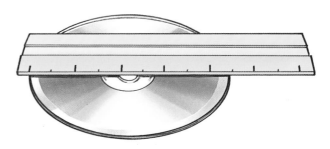

income   *noun*
Income is the **money** that a **company** or a person **receives**. A person who has a **job** will receive **wages** or a **salary**, and may also **earn interest** on a **bank account**. These are all forms of income. A company will receive income from **selling goods** or **services** to its **customers**. Another word for income is revenue.
His income during January was $2,000.

income tax   *noun*
Income tax is a **tax paid** by people and **companies** on what they **earn**. Income taxes are usually structured so that the **percentage** of tax **increases** as **income** rises.
He paid $2,500 in income tax last year.

increase   *verb*
To increase is to get bigger.
The amount of water in the pond increased after the rain.

index   (plural **indexes** or **indices**)   *noun*
1. Index is another word for **power**.
In 2^3 the index of 2 is 3.
2. An index is a **number** used to **measure** changes in a country's **economy**. For example, The **Financial Times Index** measures the change in prices on the London **Stock Exchange**.
A Consumer Price Index measures the change in price of everyday goods and services.

Indian rupee   *noun*
The Indian rupee is the **currency** of India. The rupee is divided into 100 paise.

industry   *noun*
Industry is a general term that refers to **manufacturing** activity. Often the word refers to a group of **companies** making similar **products**, for example the steel industry or the automobile industry.
The construction industry is in trouble because few new houses are being built.
industrial   *adjective*

inequality   *noun*
Inequality means that two or more **numbers** have different **values**. Inequalities are like **equations**, but they use a greater-than sign (>) or a less-than sign (<) instead of an equal sign (=). The inequality 5 > 4 means that 5 is greater than 4.
The inequality 3 < 7 means 3 is less than 7.

infinity   *noun*
Infinity means something without an end. It is represented by the **symbol** ∞. In a **series** of **numbers**, is often used to show that the list can continue forever.
The set of numbers can be written 0, 2, 4, 6, 8, 10, 12, ∞.
infinite   adjective

inflation   ► page 69

ingot   *noun*
An ingot is a mass of metal that is made into a block or bar. It may be melted down at a later date to make other objects, such as **coins** or jewelry. **Gold**, **silver**, and other metals are formed into ingots.
They stored the gold as ingots before melting them down to make jewelry.

inheritance   *noun*
An inheritance is an amount of **money** or **goods received** as a gift upon someone's death. Inheritances are often passed to children on the death of a parent.
When their parents died, their inheritance included a house.
inherit   verb

insolvent   ► **bankrupt**

inflation *noun*

Inflation is a continual increase in prices. It is usually caused by an increase in the amount of money in **circulation**. There is more money but it can buy fewer goods and services. Hyperinflation is very severe inflation. The opposite of inflation is **deflation**.

The rate of inflation was gradually coming down.

inflationary *adjective*

All these things contribute to the price of bread.

If their cost goes up, the price of bread goes up.

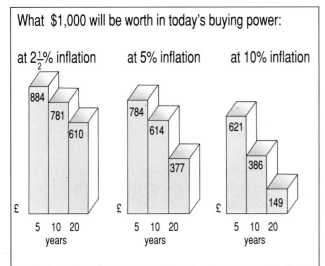

What $1,000 will be worth in today's buying power:

at 2½% inflation — 884, 781, 610 (5 10 20 years)

at 5% inflation — 784, 614, 377 (5 10 20 years)

at 10% inflation — 621, 386, 149 (5 10 20 years)

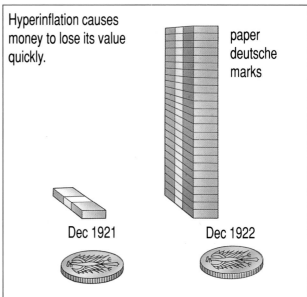

Hyperinflation causes money to lose its value quickly.

paper deutsche marks

Dec 1921   Dec 1922

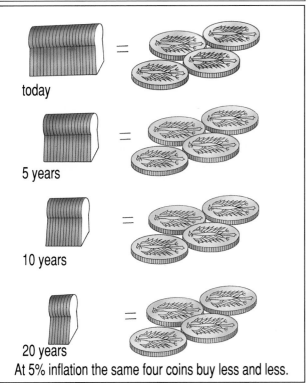

today

5 years

10 years

20 years

At 5% inflation the same four coins buy less and less.

In the space of a year, postwar German paper money became worth a fraction of what it had been worth. It required a basket of money to buy a loaf of bread.

insurance *noun*
Insurance is a **financial** arrangement people make to protect themselves from a certain event, such as the death of a family member. A regular **payment**, or **premium**, is made to an insurance **company**. With life insurance, if the insured person dies, the company will pay out a sum of **money** to his or her survivor.
The premium for the insurance policy was $500 per year.

integer *noun*
An integer is a **positive** or a **negative** whole **number**. For example, 2, 5, 9, –3, –7, and 0 are all integers. Another term for integer is whole number.
The sum of two integers is always another integer.

intercept *noun*
The intercept of a **graph** is the place where the **line** on the graph crosses one of the **axes**.
The intercept with the y-axis is at y = –2.

interest *noun*
Interest is the **price** a **lender charges** when someone **borrows money**. The lender is often a **bank**. Until the **borrower repays** the money, he or she **pays** interest at regular intervals, perhaps each **month** or each **year**.
He paid 10 percent interest on his car loan.

interior angles *plural noun*
The interior angles of a **shape** are the **angles** inside the shape which are formed when its sides meet. The interior angles of a **rectangle** are all **right angles**.
The interior angles of a triangle always add up to 180°.

international *adjective*
International describes things that affect more than one country.
The United Nations is an international organization.

International Monetary Fund ▶ IMF

interpolation *noun*
Interpolation is the working out of **numbers** that are between other numbers. If a **price** list shows the price of nails in groups of 10, the price of 25 nails can be worked out by interpolation.

Number of nails	Price in cents
10	10
20	19
30	27
40	34

The price of 25 nails was 24 cents.

intersection *noun*
1. The intersection of two **lines** on a **graph** is the place where the lines cross.
The teacher placed an X at the intersection.
2. The intersection of two **sets** of things is the collection of all the things that belong to both sets. If one set contains pencils and the other set contains green things, the intersection of the two sets is the collection of all the green pencils.
The intersection of two sets can be shown on a **Venn diagram**.
When the objects were sorted, some of them overlapped in the intersection.

Venn diagram

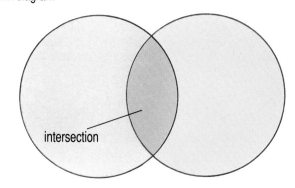

intersection

inventory *noun*
Inventory is a **stock** of **goods** waiting to be sold.
The car dealer had 40 cars in inventory.

inverse proportion   *noun*
Inverse proportion means that when one thing **increases** something else **decreases**. For example if three men take four hours to dig a garden, six men will take only two.
The time required to complete the job is in inverse proportion to the number of workers.

invert   *verb*
To invert a shape in **geometry**, is to turn it upside down or backwards. To invert a **fraction** in **mathematics** is to change the positions of the **numerator** and **denominator**.
It you invert a triangle, it looks like this.

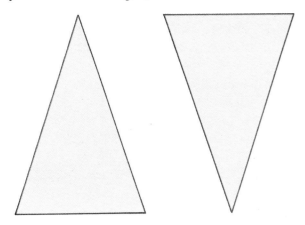

investment   *noun*
1. An investment is something on which a **business spends money** now in the hope that it will **earn** more money later on. For example, a business might invest in a new machine so that it can make its **products** more cheaply. This will help the business to **increase** its **profits** in the future.
The company plans an investment of about $2 million in new machinery next year.
2. An investment is a **financial asset** bought by an individual ora **company** in order to **earn income** from it or to make a **capital gain** on **selling** it. For example, a person might **buy shares** in a company.
Her investment in stock earned an income of $230 last year.
invest   *verb*
investor   *noun*

investment company   *noun*
An investment company is a company which uses its money to buy a wide range of **shares** and other **investments**. It will purchase from many different sources to reduce its **risk**. By choosing investments wisely, the investment company can earn a good **income** as well as increase its **capital**. Individuals can buy shares in an investment company. They are then entitled to a share of the income it produces.
He paid $2,000 to buy shares in an investment company.

invoice ▶ bill

Iraqi dinar   *noun*
The Iraqi dinar is the **currency** of Iraq.
An Iraqi dinar is worth 1,000 fils.

Irish punt   *noun*
The Irish punt is the **currency** of Ireland. There are 100 pence in a punt.

irregular shape   *noun*
An irregular shape is one in which all the sides are not of equal length, and interior angles are of different sizes.
The boundary of the city formed an irregular shape.

isosceles triangle
noun
An isosceles triangle is a **triangle** that has two 'sides the same **length**. Two of the **angles** of an isosceles triangle are equal. The name isosceles comes from the Greek word *isos* which means equal.
The tower was designed as a steep-sided isosceles triangle.

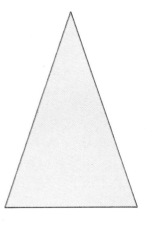

issue *noun*
An issue is an amount of **shares** or other **investments** that a **company** makes available for **purchase**.
Two thousand shares were made available by the company in the last issue.
issue *verb*

job *noun*
A job is something that has to be done. Some jobs are done to earn **money**.
A person who has a job is someone who is employed.

joint account *noun*
A joint account is an **account** at a **bank** or other institution created for the use of two or more customers. Each person named on the account can make **deposits** or **withdrawals**.
The husband and wife opened a joint account at the local bank.

joint venture *noun*
A joint venture is a **business** that is set up by two individual **companies** to sell their **goods** in a particular **market**. A joint venture is often formed when a single company does not have adequate **money** or resources or is prevented for some other reason from setting up in a market on its own. It joins forces with a second company to achieve this end. Both companies hold **stock** and make **profits** from the joint venture company.
The company set up a joint venture with a local company to make cement in Dubai.

Kenyan shilling   *noun*
The Kenyan shilling is the **currency** of Kenya. One shilling is divided into 100 cents.

kilo-   *prefix*
Kilo- is a prefix that means a thousand. It is usually shortened to *k*. A **kilogram** is 1,000 grams and is written in its short form as kg. A **kilometer**, or km, is 1,000 **meters**.
Scientists often weight things in kilograms.

kilogram   *noun*
A kilogram is a **measure** of **weight** and mass in the **metric system**. It is made up of 1,000 **grams**. A kilogram equals 2.2046 **pounds**.
One thousand kilograms equal 1 metric ton.

kilometer   *noun*
A kilometer is a **metric measure** of **length**. It is made up of 1,000 **meters**. A kilometer is equal to .6137 **miles**.
The distance they walked to school each day was one kilometer.

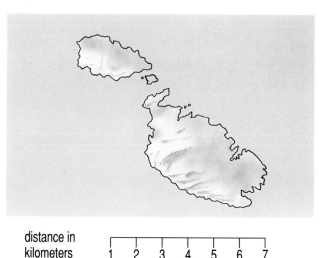

distance in kilometers   1 2 3 4 5 6 7

koruna   *noun*
The koruna is the **currency** of the Czech Republic and the Slovak Republic. It is made up of 100 haler.

krona   *noun*
The krona is the unit of **currency** of several countries, including Iceland and Sweden. In Sweden the krona is worth 100 öre. In Iceland, there are 100 aurar to one krona.

krone   *noun*
The krone is the unit of **currency** of several countries, including Norway and Denmark. In both countries, 100 øre make one krone.

krugerrand ► rand

kyat   *noun*
The kyat is the **currency** of Burma. There are 100 pyas in a kyat.

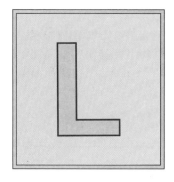

labyrinth   *noun*
A labyrinth, or maze, is a complicated pattern of passages that poses a problem of order or logic.
We got lost in the labyrinth.

landlord   *noun*
A landlord is a person or **company** who owns a building and allows someone else to live in it or do **business** in it. In return for this, the person who occupies the building **pays rent** to the landlord.
The landlord charged a monthly rent.

language   ▶ page 76

latitude   *noun*
Latitude is the **distance** north or south of the equator of a place on Earth's surface. It is **measured** in **degrees** north and degrees south. A place on the equator has latitude 0°. The North Pole has latitude 90° north.
The latitude of Philadelphia is 40° north.

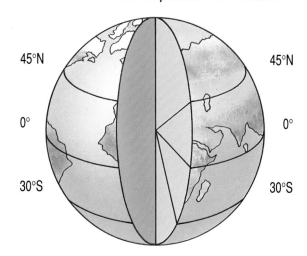

lattice   ▶ grid

leap year   *noun*
A leap year is a **year** with 366 days instead of 365 days. The extra day is added to February. Every four years, February has 29 days instead of 28.
If the last two digits of a year are divisible by 4, the year is a leap year.

lease   *noun*
A lease is a **contract** by which the owner of an **asset** allows another person to use it in exchange for regular **payments**. If a **business** cannot afford to **buy** an **expensive** asset because it does not have enough **cash**, it may be possible to obtain the use of it under a lease agreement.
The company entered into a lease agreement to obtain the use of a machine for monthly payments of $2,000.

ledger   *noun*
A ledger is a collection of **accounts**. It is a **financial** record of everything a **business** has **bought** or **sold**. The ledger may be written down in a book, or it may be held on a **computer**.
The sales ledger contains a list of the company's customers who buy goods on credit.

legal tender   *noun*
Legal tender means **coins** and **notes** that may be used to **buy** things.
In the United States, the halfpenny is no longer legal tender.

lek   *noun*
The lek is the **currency** of Albania. One lek is made up of 100 qintars.

lend   *verb*
To lend is to allow someone else to **borrow money** or **goods** that must be returned later. In **business**, lending usually means giving money to someone on condition that it be **repaid** in the future. Until the **loan** is repaid, it is normal to **pay interest** on it.
The bank will lend the company $10,000.

lender *noun*
A lender is a person or a **company** that **lends money** to people.
Banks are lenders of money.

length ► **distance**

less *adjective*
Less means not as many as, or fewer. It can also mean subtract. The **mathematical symbol** < stands for less than. The − symbol stands for subtract, or minus.
Five is less than nine written and can be written 5 < 9.

letter of credit *noun*
A letter of credit is a **guarantee**, or legal promise. It authorizes the named person or **company** to receive a certain amount of cash or credit.
Letters of credit are sometimes used to guarantee payments for exported goods.

leu (plural **lei**) *noun*
The leu is the **currency** of Romania. There are 100 bani to one leu.

lev (plural **leva**) *noun*
The lev is the **currency** of Bulgaria. The lev is **divided** into 100 stotinki.

liabilities *plural noun*
Liabilities are amounts of **money** that an individual or a **business** owes to other people. If a business **buys goods** on **credit**, it has a liability to the **company** that **supplies** the goods. If an individual **borrows** money from a **bank**, he or she has a liability to that bank. The liabilities of a business are listed on its **balance sheet.**
The company reduced its liabilities by repaying the money it owed to the bank.

line *noun*
A line is the path traced by a moving **point**. It has **length** but no width.
A pencil was used to draw a line between the two points on the map.

linear *adjective*
Linear describes a **straight line**.
The linear distance between two places on a map is the distance between them measured in a straight line.

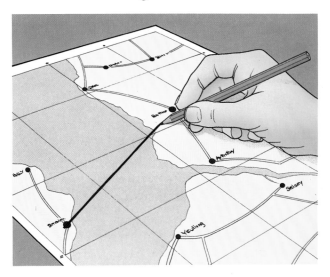

linear equation *noun*
A linear equation is a kind of **equation** used in **algebra**. An equation like $y = 2x + 3$ is called a linear equation because when it is drawn on a **graph** with y on the **vertical axis**, and x on the **horizontal** axis, it makes a **straight line**.
Linear equations are the simplest equations used in algebra.

liquid *adjective*
Liquid refers to **investments** that can easily be converted to **cash**. Bonds and **stocks** are liquid **assets**, because they can be sold readily.
Real estate is not liquid, because it may be difficult to find a purchaser.

liquidate *verb*
To liquidate means to **sell** off the **assets** of a **company** to raise **cash**. This may happen when the company is **insolvent** and cannot pay its **debts**. The **money** raised from selling off the assets is used to **pay** as much of the company's debts as possible.
The directors decided to liquidate the company.

language *noun*

The language of number refers to the names given to numbers and mathematical terms. There are around 3,000 languages in the world, and each one has its own set of words to refer to numbers.

Languages that have developed from shared origins sometimes use similar words for numbers.

The googol

Googol is the name given to a one followed by one hundred zeros. Written in full, a googol looks like 1000000000000000000000000000000000000000000000000000000000000000000000000000000000000000000000000000000000. It can be written more economically as 10^{100}. The term googolplex is used to mean ten multiplied by itself a googol times. Mathematicians find it useful to have words to refer to the huge numbers they sometimes work with.

English	Chinese	French	German	Arabic	Hindi
One	一	Un	Eins	واحِد	एक
Two	二	Deux	Zwei	إثنان	दो
Three	三	Trois	Drei	ثلاثة	तीन
Four	四	Quatre	Vier	أربعة	चार
Five	五	Cinq	Fünf	خمسة	पाँच
Six	六	Six	Sechs	سِتّة	छः
Seven	七	Sept	Sieben	سبعة	सात
Eight	八	Huit	Acht	ثمانية	आठ
Nine	九	Neuf	Neun	تسعة	नौ
Ten	十	Dix	Zehn	عشرة	दस

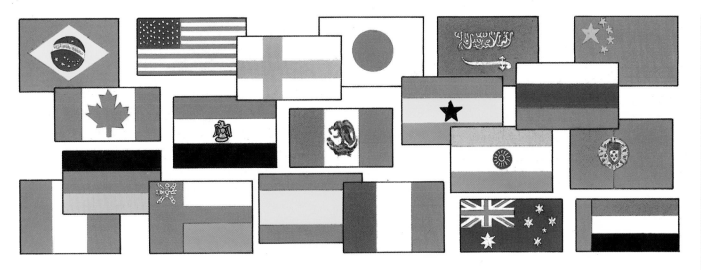

Spanish	Russian	Italian	Portugese	Ashanti
Uno	Один	Uno	Um	Eko
Dos	два	Due	Dois	Eno
Tres	три	Tre	Três	Esa
Cuatro	четыре	Quattro	Quatro	Enae
Cinco	пять	Cinque	Cinco	Innum
Seis	шесть	Sei	Seis	Insia
Siete	семь	Sette	Sete	Nso
Ocho	восемь	Otto	Oito	Inwotwi
Nueve	девять	Nove	Nove	Enkoro
Diez	десять	Dieci	Dez	Edu

lira (plural **lire**)   *noun*
The lira is the **currency** of several countries, including Italy and Turkey. The Turkish Lira is **divided** into 100 kurus or piastres.

listed company   *noun*
A listed company is a **company** whose shares are traded on a stock exchange, so that they may be freely bought and sold. Many large American corporations are listed on the New York Stock Exchange; a large British company is likely to be listed on the London Stock Exchange.
He bought 1,000 shares in a company that was listed on the New York Stock Exchange.

liter   *noun*
A liter is a **unit** of **capacity**. A liter equals slightly more than a **quart** in the **imperial system**.
In Europe, gasoline is sold by the liter.

loan   *noun*
A loan is an amount of **money** that someone **borrows**. The money has to be **paid** back. When a **bank lends** money it usually charges **interest** on the loan.
He took out a loan for $10,000 to buy a new car.

logarithm   *noun*
A logarithm is a **number** used in repeated **multiplication**. It is known as a **power**. To find the logarithm of a number its **base** must be known. The logarithm of 1000 in base 10 is 3 because 10 to the power of 3, or 10^3, = $10 \times 10 \times 10 = 1,000$.
Can you work out the logarithm 2^4?

logic   *noun*
Logic is a way of thinking in order to **solve problems**. All the facts are first gathered together and then built on to work out new facts. For example, in the diagram below, it is possible to criss-cross from one island to another using each bridge only once
Some problems in mathematics require logic to solve them.

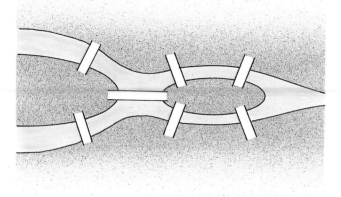

logo   *noun*
A logo is a **symbol** that a **company** uses to distinguish itself from other companies. It is often a pictorial symbol. A logo is a form of **trademark**.
The airline's red wing logo was famous all over the world.

long division   *noun*
Long division is the name given to **division** when the divider is greater than ten. The full **number** is **divided** in parts, the answer being worked from the high **value** to the lower value numbers.
Long division is used to work out $750 \div 16$.

```
        46.875
16 │ 750.000
     64
     ──
     110
      96
      ──
     140
     128
     ───
     120
     112
     ───
      80
      80
      ──
       0
```

longitude *noun*

Longitude is the **distance** east or west of a place on Earth's surface. Greenwich is a place near London, in the United Kingdom. Longitude is **measured** in **degrees** counted west or east of Greenwich, which has longitude 0°.

The Greenwich meridian is represented by a brass line on the ground at Greenwich.

long multiplication *noun*

Long multiplication is the method used to **multiply** by a **number** greater than 10. Instead of multiplying by the whole **multiplier** at once, we break it down into smaller **value** numbers that are easier to use. For example, to multiply by 256, three stages of **multiplication** are needed: multiplication by 6, by 50 and then by 200. Finally, the three totals are **added** together.

To multiply a number by 451, long multiplication is used.

loss *noun*

A loss is the amount by which the **expenditure** of a **business** is greater than its **income**. The opposite of loss is **profit**.

The company had a loss last year because sales were low.

lottery ▶ page 80

lowest common denominator *noun*

The lowest common denominator of two **numbers** is the lowest number that they both **divide** into without a **remainder**. The number 12 is the lowest number that 4 and 6 both divide into, so 12 is their lowest common denominator.

The lowest common denominator of 12 and 20 is 60.

Lydian coin *noun*

Lydian coins were the first **coins** ever made. Lydia was an area in the country now called Turkey. The coins were bean-shaped lumps of a metal called electrum, which was a mixture of **gold** and **silver**. The coins were stamped with the king's head to **guarantee** their **value**. This idea was soon adopted by **traders** from other countries and the idea spread.

Lydian coins were circulated as long ago as 545 B.C.

lottery *noun*

A lottery is a way of raising money by selling numbered tickets. Numbers are drawn at **random**, and holders of the winning tickets receive a prize. Any game in which the winner is picked at random is a kind of lottery.

He bought ten tickets in the lottery, but did not win anything.

The winning ticket must be presented to collect the prize.

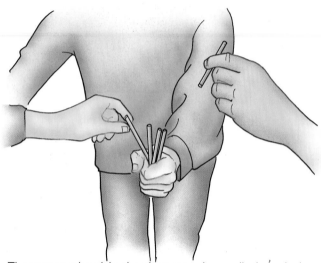

The person who picks the short straw is usually the unlucky one who has to do something. This is called choosing lots.

Numbers are mixed up in a barrel, and winning numbers are picked at random.

Some lottery tickets let you know immediately whether you have won.

Lottery tickets are often sold at newstands.

magic square ▶ page 82

magnetic strip *noun*
A magnetic strip is a strip of magnetized metal found on the back of a **credit** or **bank card**. It holds the **code** that is used to transfer information about the card owner to a machine, such as a **cash dispenser**.
The magnetic strip on the cash card had worn out, so the cash dispenser could not read it.

mail order *noun*
Mail order is a way of **buying goods** without having to go to a **store**. A mail order **company** advertises its goods in a catalog. A person who wants to buy the goods either writes to the company or telephones it. Then he or she **pays** for the goods by mailing a **money order** or **check**, or by **credit card**, and the company mails the goods to the **customer**.
She bought a new coat by mail order.

manufacturer *noun*
A manufacturer is a **company** that makes **goods**. The manufacturer will usually **sell** these goods to a **store**, which, in turn, will sell them to **customers**.
The manufacturer made sewing machines.
manufacture *verb*

magnitude *noun*
The magnitude of an object is its size. In **geometry**, **lines** and **angles** are measured by their magnitude.
The brightest stars are said to be of first magnitude.

map *noun*
A map is a drawing that represents part of Earth's surface. There are many kinds of maps. Some show whole countries, while local ones show the detailed roads in a town or smaller area. Maps of the sea are called **charts**. They show how deep the sea is so that ships can sail on a safe course.
The hikers used a map to find their way across the country.
map *verb*

mapping *noun*
Mapping is a **diagram** that shows the connection between two **sets** of **numbers**. It is also called a **function**.
They used mapping to link the individual numbers of the set together.

margin *noun*
A margin is a form of **profit**. For example, in a toystore, the margin for each toy is the difference between what a **customer pays** for the toy and what the **store** paid for it.
The margin on the toy was only a few cents once it had been reduced in the toystore sale.

mark ▶ **deutsch mark**

market (*noun*) ▶ page 84

market verb
To market is to offer something for **sale**.
The clothes company will market their new coats in April.

market research *noun*
Market research is a method of finding out what **customers** want, usually by asking individuals to reply to questions in a **survey** about what they **buy**. A **supermarket** may ask customers what kind of soup they would prefer. The supermarket can then **stock** the kind that they know customers will like.
The supermarket's market research showed that most customers would prefer to buy tomato soup.

magic square   *noun*

A magic square is a kind of **matrix**. In a magic square, each row and each column add up to the same number. Adding the numbers diagonally from corner to corner also gives the same number. A magic square can be any size.

In a 4-by-4 magic square, there are 880 different ways of arranging the numbers 1 to 16.

Rows in a 3-by-3 magic square always add up to 15. Magic squares like this were known 2,000 years ago in China.

16	3	2	13
5	10	11	8
9	6	7	12
4	15	14	1

This magic square was devised by the great German artist Albrecht Dürer. The rows all add up to 34, and the numbers in the pink squares at the bottom indicate the year Dürer made the square, 1514.

marketing *noun*
Marketing is a way of making a potential **buyer** aware that a **product** is available. It is usually done by people involved with **sales**. Marketing may involve making a brochure or creating some kind of eye-catching display.
The company is marketing new windows by using an outdoor display.

markka *noun*
The markka is the **currency** of Finland. It is made up of 100 pennies.

mathematics *noun*
Mathematics is the science of **numbers**. It is the study of **patterns**, **measurements**, and relationships between numbers. Branches of mathematics include **algebra**, **arithmetic**, **calculus**, **geometry**, **logic**, **statistics**, and **trigonometry**.
Mathematics is a complex science.

matrix (plural **matrixes** or **matrices**) *noun*
A matrix is a **set** of **numbers** arranged in a **rectangle**. It is like a **numerical table** and is used to organize large amounts of information and make them easier to read and understand. The output from a **spreadsheet** is a kind of matrix.
They used a matrix to show how many and what kinds of cars were sold in the country.

maximum *noun*
The maximum of a **set** of **numbers** is the largest number in it. The maximum of the set 2, 6, 4, 8, 1, 3 is 8.
The maximum number of people you can carry in the elevator is 12.

maze ► **labyrinth**

mean ► **average**

measure verb
To measure is to find out the **size** or extent of something. To measure is to see how big or how heavy something is. **Lengths** can be measured in **feet**, and **weights** can be measured in **pounds**.
Angles are measured in degrees using a protractor.

measurement ► page 86

median *noun*
1. Median means middle. If a **set** of **numbers** is sorted in order of **size**, the median of the numbers is the middle one in the **sequence**. The median of 2, 4, 6, 7, 9, 12, 25 is 7.
They took the July temperature in Morocco as a median guide.
2. The median is a line drawn from the **vertex**, or **apex**, of a triangle to the midpoint of the opposite side.
The median divided the base of the scalene triangle.

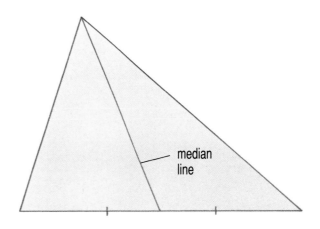
median line

market *noun*

1. A market is a place where people buy and sell things.

She sold eggs from a stall in the market.

2. The market can also describe a group of buyers who are likely to be most interested in buying a particular product or range of products. For example, a market might refer to the group of young people under 21 years of age.

The designer presented new ideas for the children's toy market.

A street seller offers goods from his bicycle.

The shelves are well stocked in a supermarket.

There are many different stalls in a souk.

Merchants sell goods from their boats in a floating market.

A roadside stall sells traditional medicines.

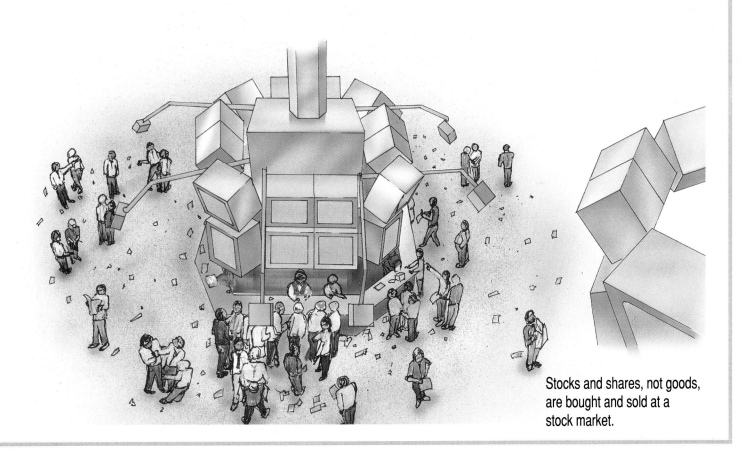

Stocks and shares, not goods, are bought and sold at a stock market.

measurement *noun*

A measurement is a way of finding out the size, weight, or extent of something. Measurements are made according to a scale of **units**. The base units in the SI **metric system** of measurement are the meter to measure length, the kilogram for weight or mass, the second for time, and the kelvin for temperature.

He made a careful measurement of the doorframe to make sure that he had enough wood to fix it.

Volume
In the metric system, the volume of liquid is measured in liters.

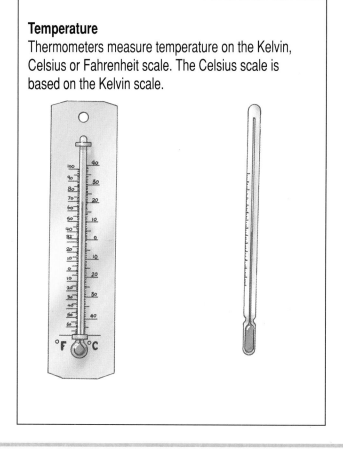

Size
In the metric system, length, area, and volume are measured in meters.

Temperature
Thermometers measure temperature on the Kelvin, Celsius or Fahrenheit scale. The Celsius scale is based on the Kelvin scale.

Weight or mass

A metal cylinder weighing exactly one kilogram is the standard for all metric units of weight and mass. The cylinder is kept in France.

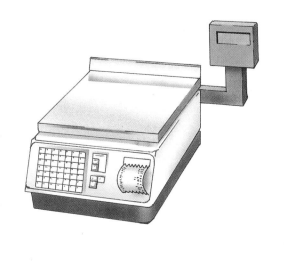

Other pieces of equipment make different measurements

watch measures time

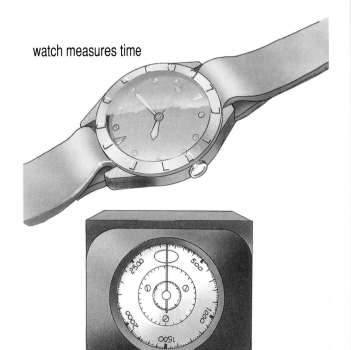

altimeter measures height

speedometer measures speed

barometer measures air pressure

member   *noun*
A member is an object or value that belongs to a **set**. If there is a group of cups, each cup is a member of the set of cups.
The parachute club had 24 members.

merchandise   *noun*
Merchandise refers to things that are bought and sold. The **products** that are offered in a **store** are its merchandise. A synonym for merchandise is **goods**.
The week before Christmas, the children stood in front of the store windows, admiring all the merchandise on display.

merchant ► **trader**

merger   *noun*
A merger is the joining together of two or more **companies** to form a single company. Two companies that carry on the same kind of **business** might join forces to try to get a bigger share of the **market**.
The two companies expect to make bigger profits because of the merger.

mesh ► **net**

meter   *noun*
A meter is a metric **unit** of **length**. It is used to **measure** how long, wide, or high something is. A meter equals 39.37 **inches**.
The hedge was two meters high.
metric   *adjective*

metric system   *noun*
The metric system is a **set** of **units** used for **measurement**. The three main units are the **gram**, which measures **weight**, the **meter**, which measures **length**, and the **liter**, which measures **capacity**. Each unit **increases** by tens.
The metric system is used in many countries.

metric ton   *noun*
A metric ton is a **unit** of **weight**. It is equal to 1,000 **kilograms**, or about 2,200 **pounds**.
The automobile weighed one metric ton.

Mexican peso   *noun*
The Mexican peso is the **currency** of Mexico.

mile   *noun*
A mile is an **imperial measure** of **length**. A mile **measures** 1,760 **yards** (5,280 **feet**) and is equal to 1.61 **kilometers**.
He walked several miles before becoming tired.

milli-   *prefix*
Milli- is a prefix that means one thousandth. A millimeter is a thousandth of a **meter**, so there are 1,000 millimeters in a meter.
The bottle contained only 16 milliliters of water.

milligram   *noun*
A milligram is a **metric measure** of **weight** in the **metric system**. There are 1,000 milligrams in a **gram**. It equals about two millionths of a **pound**.
The powder grams were measured in milligrams.

milliliter   *noun*
A milliliter is a **metric measure** of **volume** in the **metric system**. There are 1,000 milliliters in a **liter**. A millileter is equal to 0.061 **cubic inches**.
There were 200 milliliters of liquid in the tube.

millimeter   *noun*
A millimeter is a **metric measure** of **length** in the **metric system**. There are 1,000 millimeters in a **meter**. A millimeter is equal to 0.03937 **inches**.
The insect measured only a few millimeters in length.

milling *noun*

Milling is the small grooves on the edges of some **coins**. When coins were made of smooth disks of real **gold**, people were able to tamper with the **shape** and scrape a little of the gold off the edge of the coin. Milling was invented so that any scraping could be easily seen.

Although most modern coins are not made of gold, many still have milling.

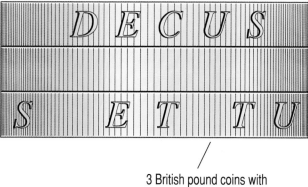

3 British pound coins with milled edges

million *noun*

A million is a thousand thousands. It is written 1,000,000.

The country's population was 75 million.

millionaire *noun*

A millionaire is a person who has a million **units** of **currency**. In the United States, a millionaire has a million **dollars**.

The British millionaire had a million pounds.

minimum *noun*

The minimum is the smallest, or least, amount. The minimum of a **set** of **numbers** is the smallest number in the set. The minimum of the set 2, 6, 4, 8, 1, 3 is 1.

The minimum temperature tonight will be 5°F.

mint ▶ page 92

minus sign *noun*

Minus is the sign (−) used to indicate that the number following it is a **negative number** or is to be **subtracted** from the number before the sign.

Temperatures with a minus sign are cold.

minute *noun*

1. A minute is a **unit** of **time**. There are 60 **minutes** in an **hour**. **Clock** makers **divided** the hour into 60 minutes when clocks became accurate enough to need smaller units than the **hour**.

It took 10 minutes to walk to school.

2. A minute is a **unit** of an **angle**. It is one-sixtieth of a **degree**.

A circle is divided into 360 parts called degrees, with each degree divided into 60 minutes.

miser *noun*

A miser is a person who saves **money** and will not **spend** it. The opposite of a miser is a **spendthrift**.

The miser would not give any money to charity.

mixed number *noun*

A mixed number consists of a **whole number** and a **fraction** together. $3\frac{3}{4}$ and $4\frac{5}{9}$ are both mixed numbers.

He changed an improper fraction into a mixed number.

Mobius strip *noun*

A Mobius strip is a strip of material that is given a one-half twist and joined at the ends. It therefore has only one side and stays in one piece when it is split down the middle.

A Mobius strip has interesting geometric properties.

mint *noun*

A mint is a place where coins are made. The government carefully controls the making of coins. The mint is also used to store coins before they go into circulation. When coins are minted, they are counted into bags by machine. A label is attached to show how many coins there are and of what **denomination**. They are then taken to a stronghold ready for dispatch.
They made quarters at the mint.

An artist makes a large model of a British pound coin.

This electrotype copy is put on a reducing machine. It is scanned in a spiral by a tracer. The tracer movements are conducted by a bar to a rotating cutter. The cutter copies each movement, at the size of the finished coin. It is cutting into a block of steel. This steel copy is the master punch, with the features of the coin in relief. The master punch is used to make working punches, that are used to make working dies. The details are gone over to get rid of any flaws and the working dies are polished.

A mold of the model is placed in an electroplating bath. Nickel and then copper are deposited on it.

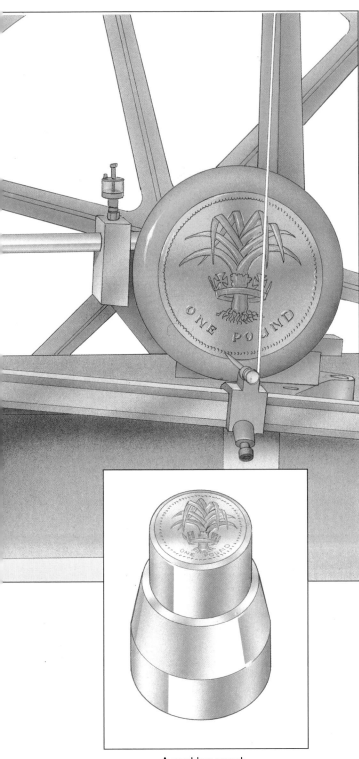

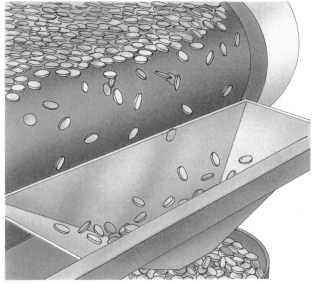

Blank coins are softened by passing them through a furnace.

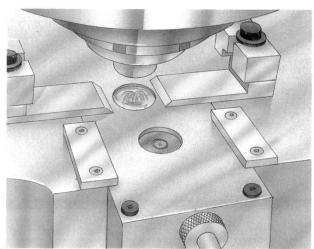

The head and tail design are stamped onto the blank at the same time. A collar holds the blank in place.

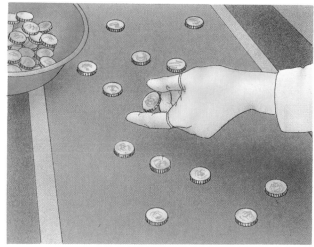

A working punch.

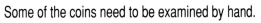

Some of the coins need to be examined by hand.

mode   *noun*
The mode of a **set** of **numbers** is the number that is most frequent. The mode of the set 3, 6, 4, 8, 6, 4, 3, 4, 9 is 4, because there are more 4s than any other number.
To find out the most common shoe size, the shop manager worked out the mode of all the sizes.

model ▶ page 93

modulus   *noun*
Modulus is the absolute **value** of a **number**, or its value regardless of any signs it may have around it. The modulus of a **positive number** is the number itself, so the modulus of 4 is 4. The modulus of a **negative number** is the number without the minus sign, so the modulus of −5 is 5. The modulus is always a positive number.
They worked out the modulus of −6 to be 6.

monetary policy   *noun*
Monetary policy is the plan of action taken by a government to influence the way a country's **economy** operates. It usually involves controlling the amount of **money** in **circulation**, as well as **credit** and **interest rates**. Monetary policy is used to help the economy grow, to keep as many people as possible **employed**, and to keep **prices** and **wages** at a favorable level.
The government changed its monetary policy in order to help the country out of recession.

money   *noun*
Money means any **coins**, **notes**, **checks** or other things that can be used to **buy goods** or **services**. Beads, cocoa beans, shells, and stones are some of the things that have been used as money in the past. **Silver** and **gold** were used more widely. They were the main forms of money because they were convenient and hardwearing.
He does not have enough money to go on vacation.
monetary   *adjective*

money order   *noun*
A money order is an **order** for the **company** or institution that **issues** it to **pay** a certain amount of **money** on **demand**. The money is paid to the person whose name is written on the order. Money orders are sold by **banks**, post offices, and some other **commercial businesses**.
Their grandmother gave them money orders for their birthdays.

monopoly   *noun*
A monopoly is exclusive control, as when a **product** or **service** is available only from one **company**. A monopoly often allows a company to **charge** high **prices**.
The opposite of monopoly is competition.

month   *noun*
A month is a **unit** of **time**. The **year** is **divided** into 12 months, although not all the months are of the same length.
A month is based on the time it takes for the moon to revolve around Earth.

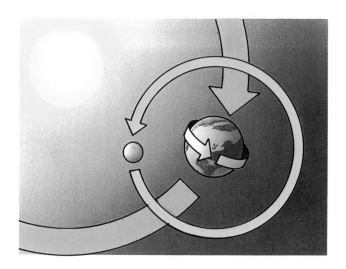

mortgage   *noun*
A mortgage is an amount of **money** given as a **loan** to **buy** a building or land. It is usually provided by a **bank**. Mortgage **repayments** are made up of the money **borrowed** plus **interest**. The mortgage is paid back every **month** for many **years**.
Their mortgage was repaid over 25 years.

model *noun*

A model is a mathematical projection or design. Combinations of numbers or a **formula** can also be used as models. A scale model is an exact copy of something reproduced in a smaller or larger size. The scale is usually given as a **ratio**. Computers are often used to build models of things that change or move, because of the high number of mathematical calculations needed to describe them.

Scientists do not know what an atom really looks like, so they use models to explain how atoms behave.

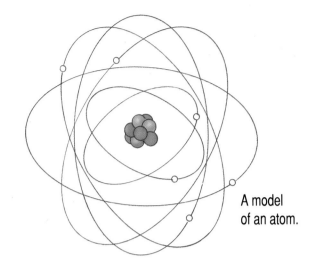

A model of an atom.

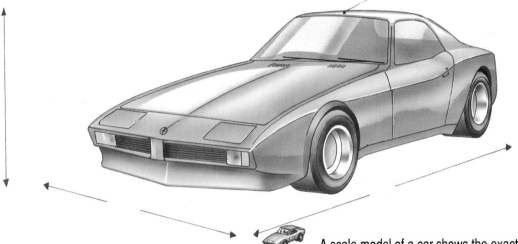

A scale model of a car shows the exact dimensions of the original. It is projected mathematically.

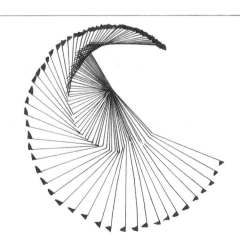

This computer model shows the exact movement of the golfer using a graphic image.

multinational *adjective*
Multinational describes a **company** that has branches in more than one country.
The multinational company opened a new branch in Peru.

multiples *plural noun*
The multiples of a **number** are all the whole numbers into which it will **divide** exactly.
He discovered the first 5 multiples of 3 were 6, 9, 12, 15, 18.

multiplicand *noun*
The multiplicand in a **multiplication problem** is the **number** that is being multiplied by the multiplier.
In the sum 426 × 8, 426 is the multiplicand.

multiplication *noun*
Multiplication is a type of **arithmetic**. The sign for multiplication is ×. Multiplication is a short way of **adding** groups of **numbers** together. If you want to add four packages of five cookies each, you can write it as 4 × 5 = 20. This is the same as adding four groups of five together.
They used multiplication to figure out how many eggs were in five boxes of one dozen each.
multiply *verb*

multiplier *noun*
The multiplier in a **multiplication problem** is the multiplying **number**. It is the second number in the problem.
In 426 × 8, 8 is the multiplier.

naira *noun*
The naira is the currency of Nigeria. There are 100 kobo in a naira.

nano- *prefix*
Nano- means one-billionth. A nanosecond is a billionth of a **second**, for example, and a nanometer is a billionth of a **meter**.
The prefix nano- is used in the metric system.

national *adjective*
National means having to do with a single nation as a whole. The opposite of national is **international**.
The president and Congress set the national budget every year.

national debt *noun*
The national debt of a country is the total amount of **money** a government owes. The level of the **debt** depends on how much the government has **borrowed**, and on how much of its borrowing it is able to **pay** back. Money to pay the national debt may be drawn from the nation's **reserves**, or from **taxes**.
The country's national debt increased as the government borrowed more money to pay for imports.

natural number *noun*
A natural number is a **positive integer**. 1, 2, 3, 4, 5, and 6 are natural numbers. Other names for natural numbers are whole numbers or positive numbers.
Natural numbers are always positive numbers.

negative number   *noun*
A negative number is a **number** that is **less** than **zero**. **Adding** a negative number to a **positive number** always **reduces** the **value** of the positive number. For example, –3 is a negative number.
The sum of two negative numbers is always negative.

negotiable   *adjective*
If a document is negotiable, it means that it can be legally passed to another person.
A check is negotiable once it's endorsed.

negotiate   *verb*
To negotiate is to form an agreement over a possible **deal**. In **business**, a salesperson might negotiate the **price** of certain **goods** with a **buyer**.
They sat around the table ready to negotiate the terms of the contract.

nest egg   *noun*
A nest egg is an amount of **money** saved for the future; it's another word for savings.
The couple had a retirement nest egg.

net *(noun)* ▶ page 96

net   adjective
Net describes the **value** of something after any necessary **deductions** have been made. If a **product** has a **price** of 60 pesos, but the **seller** offers a **discount** of 5 pesos, then the net price is 55 pesos. If someone's **wages** are $200 per **week**, but the **employer** deducts $40 for **taxes**, the net **pay** is $160.
After deducting taxes, the company was left with a net profit of $1.5 million.

net profit   *noun*
Net profit is the amount of **profit earned** by a **business** after all **expenditures** have been deducted. It will always be less than the **gross profit**.
The gross profit earned by the company was $35,000, but the net profit was only $10,000.

new sol   *noun*
The new sol is the **currency** of Peru.

New Zealand dollar   *noun*
The New Zealand dollar is the **currency** of New Zealand. It is made up of 100 cents.

nickel   *noun*
A nickel is a **coin** used in the United States. It is worth five **cents**.

Nikkei Average Price Index   *noun*
The Nikkei Average Price Index is a **number** used to indicate the movement of **share prices**, on the Tokyo Nikkei Stock Exchange. It uses the prices of the top 100 shares and changes minute by minute as share dealing takes place.
The Nikkei Average Price Index shot up as investors purchased more and more shares.

Norwegian krone   *noun*
The Norwegian krone is the **currency** of Norway. It is made up of 100 öre.

note ▶ bank note

number   *noun*
A number is a **symbol** or a word showing a **quantity**. The number of candies in a bag can be determined by **counting** them.
The number of wheels on a car is 4.
numerical   adjective

numeral ▶ page 98

net *noun*

A net, or mesh, is the name given to a flat **shape** that will form a **three-dimensional** object when it is fixed together in the right way. Nets are useful for dressmaking, making boxes for packaging, or for making **models**.

He used the net to make a pyramid for the Egyptian display.

glue tab
fold
cut

a cube

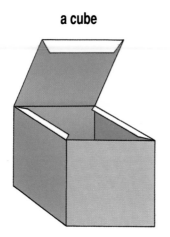

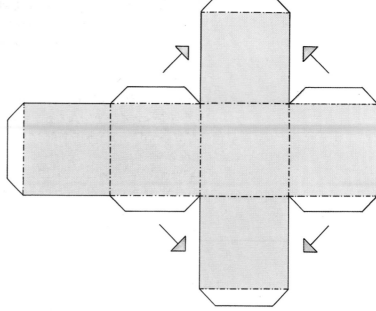

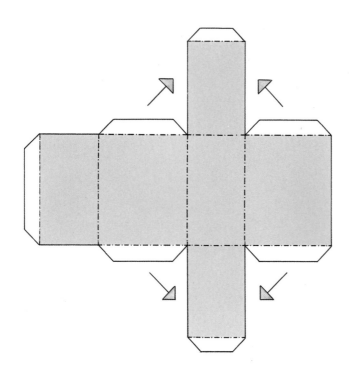

glue tab
fold
cut

a cuboid

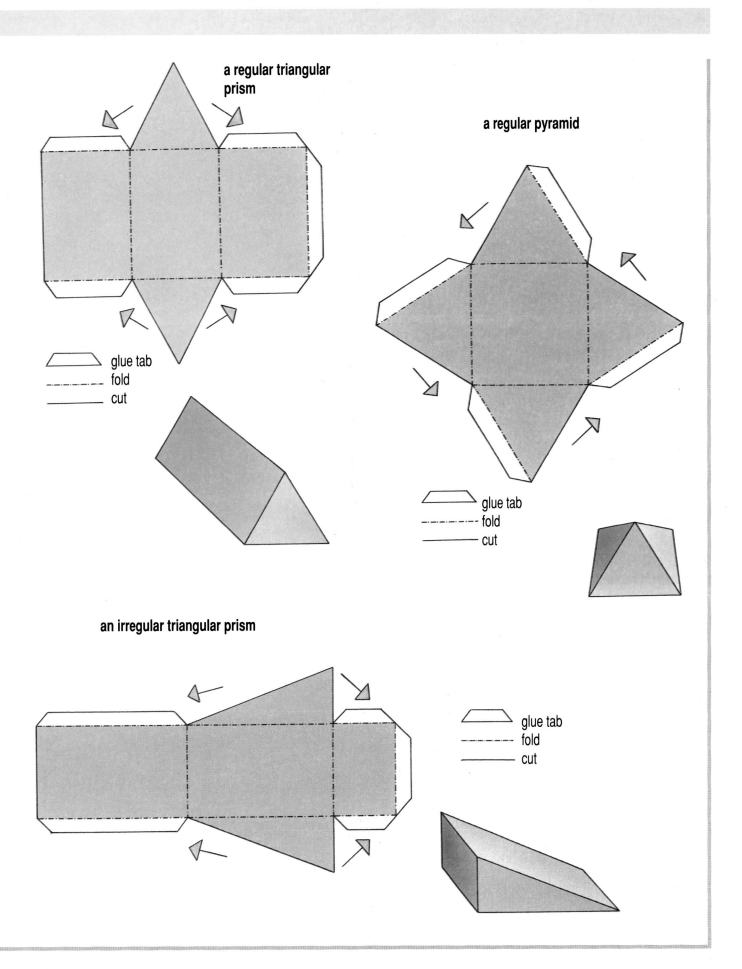

a regular triangular prism

glue tab
fold
cut

a regular pyramid

glue tab
fold
cut

an irregular triangular prism

glue tab
fold
cut

numeral   *noun*

A numeral is a symbol that stands for a number. Numerals are grouped in various ways to make a numeral system, such as the **decimal system**, that enables people to make calculations. People have written numerals in different ways in different cultures.

The numerals used to number the pages in this book are known as Hindu-Arabic numerals.

Roman numerals are often used on a clock face.

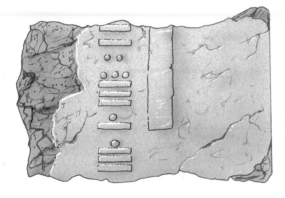

The Mayan Indians wrote groups of numerals vertically, working to base 20.

1	2	3	4	5	6	7	8	9	10	
1	**2**	**3**	**4**	**5**	**6**	**7**	**8**	**9**	**10**	Hindu-Arabic
▼	▼▼	▼▼▼	▼▼▼▼	▼▼▼▼▼	▼▼▼ / ▼▼▼	▼▼▼▼ / ▼▼▼	▼▼▼▼ / ▼▼▼▼	▼▼▼▼▼ / ▼▼▼▼	◄	Babylonian
Α	Β	Γ	Δ	Ε	Ζ	Η	Θ	Ι	Κ	Greek
I	II	III	IV	V	VI	VII	VIII	IX	X	Roman
一	二	三	四	五	六	七	八	九	十	Chinese
•	••	•••	••••	▬	•̲	••̲	•••̲	••••̲	▬̲	Mayan Indian
१	२	३	४	५	६	७	८	९	१०	Hindu

98

numerator   *noun*
The numerator of a **fraction** is the **number** above the line. It is the number that is being **divided** by the number below the line.
The numerator of the fraction $\frac{4}{7}$ is 4.

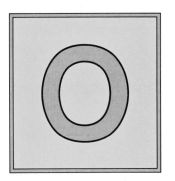

oak tree shilling   *noun*
An oak tree shilling was a **coin** used in the North American colonies of Great Britain before the United States was created. It was stamped with a picture of an oak tree.

oblong   *noun*
An oblong is another name for a **rectangle**.
The shape of a football field is oblong.

obtuse angle   *noun*
An obtuse angle is an **angle** that is larger than 90° but smaller than 180°.
The scissors opened fully to make an obtuse angle.

octagon   *noun*
An octagon is an eight-sided **polygon**.
The interior angles of a regular octagon measure 135°.

octahedron   *noun*
An octahedron is a **solid shape** that has eight faces.
An octahedron is a polyhedron.

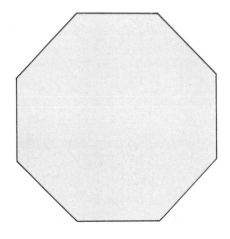

odd number   *noun*
An odd number is a **number** that cannot be **divided** exactly by 2. For example, 3, 7, 11, and 23 are odd numbers because when divided by 2 there is always a **remainder**. A number that can be divided exactly by 2 is an **even number**.
The sum of two odd numbers is always an even number.

odds   *plural noun*
Odds are an estimate of how likely it is that something will happen. At a horse race, people can bet on which horse will win. If the odds are 4 to 1 and the horse wins, those people will win four times as much **money** as they placed on the bet.
The teacher asked them to work out the odds of rolling eight with a pair of dice.

opposite angles   *plural noun*
Opposite angles are **angles** formed when two **straight lines** cross. The angles directly across from each other are opposite angles.
Opposite angles are always the same size.

order   *verb*
To order something means to ask someone to obtain it. Bookstores do not keep every book that is published because there is not enough space to do so. If a **customer** wants a book that is not in **stock**, the store will order it.
The store ordered ten more televisions.
order   *noun*

ordered pair   *noun*
An ordered pair of **numbers** is two numbers that must be written in a certain way to present the correct information. On a grid, for example, the ordered pair (3, 7) would not show the same **point** as the ordered pair (7, 3). In **graph** work **coordinates** are ordered pairs. The first number refers to a position on the **horizontal axis** and the second refers to a point on the **vertical** axis.
Find the ordered pairs 3,2 and 2,3 on the graph.

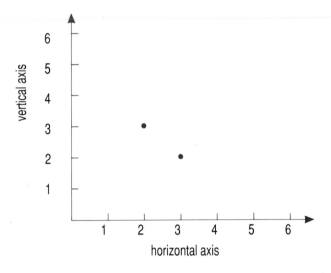

ordinary number ► **scalar**

organization   *noun*
An organization is a group of people who work, meet, or play together, usually with some shared interest or common goal in mind.
A company is one particular type of organization.

ounce   *noun*
An ounce is an **imperial measure** of either **weight** or **volume**. There are 16 ounces in one **pound**. An ounce is equivalent to approximately 28 **grams**. There are also 16 fluid ounces in one **pint**. The abbreviation of ounce is oz.
She weighed 10 ounces of flour on the scale.

oval *noun*
An oval is a kind of **curve**. It is the **shape** of a flattened **circle** or **ellipse**.
His drawing of an egg was oval.
ovoid *adjective*

overdraft *noun*
An overdraft is a form of **loan**. **Customers** can ask a **bank** if they can **borrow** a **sum** of **money** above the amount in their **account**. If the bank agrees, it may **charge interest** on the overdraft.
The bank gave him an overdraft so that he could pay for his vacation.
overdraw *verb*

Pakistani rupee *noun*
The Pakistani rupee is the **currency** of Pakistan. It is made up of 100 paisas.

paper money ► page 102

parabola *noun*
A parabola is a kind of **curve**. You can make a parabola if you slice through a **cone parallel** to its side. The lip of the cone is the **shape** of a parabola where it has been cut.
A parabola was drawn to show how the ball traveled through the air.

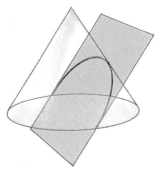

parallel *adjective*
Parallel describes two **straight lines** that never meet, however long they are. Parallel lines are always the same **distance** apart. Railroad tracks are parallel lines.
They drew a line parallel to the edge of the pavement.

parallelogram *noun*
A parallelogram is any four-sided, or **quadrilateral**, **shape** in which opposite sides are **parallel**. A rhombus is a parallelogram.
Parallelograms were used to form the mosaic.

paper money *noun*

Paper money is **currency** that is printed on paper. The Chinese were the first people to use paper money instead of coins, perhaps as long ago as AD 600. **Bank notes**, **bills of exchange**, and treasury notes are all different types of paper money. Today, many countries are replacing low-**denomination** paper money with coins. The cost of printing paper money and the length of time it lasts make it more economical to **mint** coins.
Bank tellers keep paper money separate from the coins.

China was the first country to have paper money.

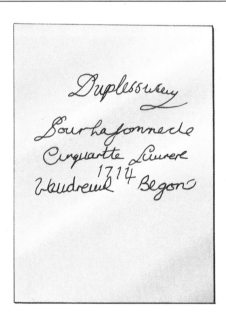

Playing cards were sometimes used as money in Canada in the late 1600s and early 1700s. The card had to be signed by the governor before it could be used as currency.

102

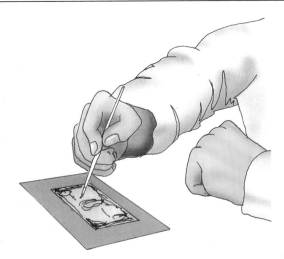

An artist designs the note.

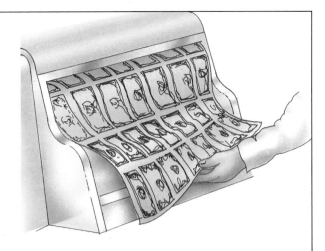

The notes are printed in sheets. Special paper and inks are used.

An engraving is made on a steel plate.

The sheets are inspected for flaws, and cut to size.

Every detail must be exact before the plates are used for printing.

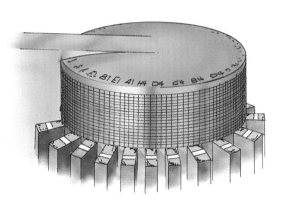

The bills are stacked and counted by machine.

parity   *noun*
Parity means equality in **value**. Another way of saying two things have parity is to say they are "at par." Two **currencies** are at parity if they are worth the same. For many years the Irish punt and the British pound shared the same value.
The punt and the pound sterling were at parity.

pattern   *noun*
In **geometry**, pattern is a design created when a particular **shape** or group of shapes is repeated a number of times. The shapes can be repeated by translation, or they can be **rotated**. A pattern is often called a design.
A pattern was used to decorate the school wall.

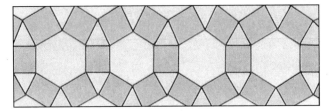

pawnbroker   *noun*
A pawnbroker is a person who **lends money**. For example, a **customer** could **borrow** $50 against a **possession** that has a higher **value**. The customer pawns the possession for **cash**. The pawnbroker will **charge interest** on the money while the **goods** are held. The pawnbroker will return the goods to their owner only if the money and interest are **repaid**.
The pawnbroker lent him a $100 in exchange for his gold watch.

payment   *noun*
Payment is **money** given to someone in exchange for **goods** or **services**. A **business** might make a payment to an electricity **company** for **supplying** power. It will also make a weekly or monthly payment to its **employees** in return for work done.
The payments made by the company last month totalled $85,000.
pay   *verb*

penniless   *adjective*
Penniless describes someone who does not have a cent of money.
The thief stole her purse and left her penniless.

penny   *noun*
A penny is a **coin** in the United States and in Britain that is not worth very much. In the United States, a penny is a **cent**. There are 100 pennies, or cents, in a **dollar**. In Britain, there are 100 pennies, or pence, in a **pound sterling**.
The child saved up her pennies in a piggy bank.

pension   *noun*
A pension is **money paid** to people after they retire from their **jobs**. Sometimes the pension is paid by person's **employer**. In some countries the pension is paid by the government.
The telephone operator retired at 65 years of age and collected a pension.

pentagon   *noun*
A pentagon is a flat **shape**, or **polygon**, that has five sides.
The interior angles of a regular pentagon are all equal to 108°.

pentagram   *noun*
A pentagram is a five-pointed star.
They used a pentagram as the logo of their company.

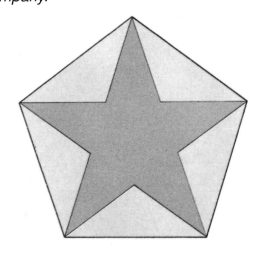

per annum   *adverb*
Per annum means each **year**. An **employee** who gets $25,000 every year is said to **earn** $25,000 per annum.
The borrower paid interest of $1,000 per annum.

percent   *adverb*
Percent means a **fraction**, or part, of a hundred. Sixty percent means sixty hundredth or $\frac{60}{100}$. If 60 percent of people like chocolate, it means that 60 people out of every 100 like chocolate. The **symbol** for percent is %.
Seventy-five percent of the crowd cheered for the home team.
percentage   *noun*

percentile   *noun*
A percentile is any one of the 100 **equal** groups into which a large group of things or people has been **divided**.
Her perfect math score put her in the top percentile.

perimeter   *noun*
The perimeter of a flat **shape** is the **distance** around its edge. For example, the perimeter of a **hexagon** is **computed** by **adding** together the **lengths** of all six sides.
They walked around the perimeter of the playing field.

permutation   *noun*
A permutation is a rearrangement of a **set** of things in adifferent order. The set of **numbers** 1 3 5 7 9 is one permutation of 3 7 5 1 9.
They made a permutation of their combination lock by changing the order of its digits.

perpendicular   adjective
Perpendicular describes **lines** that meet at 90°. Lines that are formed at **right angles** to a **base** line are said to be perpendicular.
Vertical lines are perpendicular to horizontal lines.

peseta   *noun*
The peseta is the **currency** of Spain.

peso   *noun*
The peso is the **unit** of **currency** of several countries of the world, including Mexico, Colombia, Cuba, and the Philippines. It is **divided** into 100 cents, or centavos.

petty cash   *noun*
Petty cash is a small amount of **money** held by a **business** in the form of **notes** and **coins**. It is used to **buy** small items such as postage stamps.
The business spent $23 from petty cash.

pi   *noun*
Pi is the name given to a **number** that equals the **circumference** of a **circle** **divided** by its **diameter**. Pi is always the same for any circle and is **calculated** as 3.14159 to six **significant figures**.
The symbol for pi is π.

pictogram   *noun*
A pictogram is a **graph** that uses small **symbols** to represent information.
He used a pictogram to show how many hamburgers he had sold.

105

piece of eight   *noun*
A piece of eight was a **coin** once used in Spain and its colonies. A piece of eight was worth eight rials.

pie chart   *noun*
A pie chart is a **circle** that has been **divided** into **sectors**. The sectors are the same **shape** as slices of a pie. Each sector represents a part or **fraction** of the whole pie.
The pie chart showed how many visitors came from each European country.

piggy bank   *noun*
A piggy bank is a small hollow model of a pig. **Money** is put in through a slot in the top to encourage children to save.
She had $4 in her piggy bank.

pine tree shilling   *noun*
A pine tree shilling was a **coin** used in the North American colonies of Great Britain, before the United States was created. It had the image of a pine tree stamped on it.

pint   *noun*
A pint is a **measure** of **capacity** in the **imperial system**. It is equal to **half** a **quart** or one-eighth of a **gallon**.
They each drank a pint of milk.

place value   *noun*
Place value is a **measure** of how much a **digit** is worth according to its position within a **number**. In the number 372, the 3 is worth 300, the 7 is worth 70, and the 2 is worth 2. If these are **added** together the whole number is worth 300 + 70 + 2 = 372.
The place value of 6 in 62 is worth 60.

plane   *noun*
A plane is a flat **surface**, such as a sheet of paper. It is **two-dimensional**. Any **point** on the plane needs two **coordinates** to locate it, those of **length** and width.
The machine had to be positioned on a horizontal plane so it wouldn't move.

plane figure   *noun*
A plane figure is a **shape** with only two dimensions, **length** and width.
A square is a plane figure but a cube is a solid.

plot   *verb*
To plot is to mark **points** on a **chart**, **grid**, or **graph**. When **results** are plotted, they can be written as **coordinates** on a graph or chart, so that information can be read more easily.
The navigator plotted a course on his map.

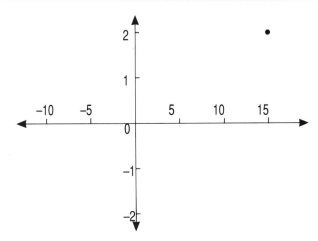

plumbline   *noun*
A plumbline is a length of string attached to a weight. The weight pulls the string downward and holds it straight. The plumbline can then be used to check whether an edge or line is **vertical** to the base line.
They used a plumbline to check that the corner post was vertical.

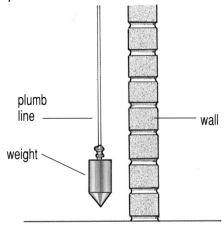

plus *preposition*
Plus means **added** to. It is represented by the **symbol** +.
We figured out that six plus eight came to fourteen.

P.M. *abbreviation*
P.M. or p.m. stands for the Latin words, *post meridiem*, which mean "after midday." P.M. is used to indicate **time** that falls in the afternoon and evening between 12 o'clock midday and 12 o'clock midnight.
Her train was scheduled to depart from the station at 6 p.m.

pocket calculator ► **calculator**

pocket money *noun*
Pocket money is an allowance that parents give their children. The children can usually **spend** the **money** as they like, or they can save it.
She got $5 pocket money each week.

point *noun*
1. A point is a position on a **map** or **graph**.
He knew where the point was by its coordinates.
2. A point is a dot that comes after the whole **number** in a **decimal** number. The decimal number 3.4 means $3\frac{4}{10}$. The decimal point tells us that the whole number is 3 and that the 4 is in the tenths **place**.
In 34.67, the decimal point comes after the 4.
3. A point is a sharp corner, such as the tip of one arm of a **star**.
A pentagram is a star with five points.

point of sale *noun*
A point of sale is a place in a **store** where **goods** are **paid** for. Most large stores install **computer** equipment at the point of sale. Each item has a **bar code**, which is used to register the **price** of the item in the computer.
She paid for the gardening book at the point of sale.

policy *noun*
1. A policy is a decision, often made by a **business** or government, that it will carry out its activities in a particular way.
It is the company's policy to pay bonuses to the staff at Christmas.
2. A policy is an agreement between an **insurance company** and a **client** that the company will **pay** out **money** as **compensation** if certain things occur. In most cases, these occurrences refer to **theft**, injury, or death. The policy is written down in a document that states what must occur before the company will pay out any money to the client.
The policy said that $100,000 would be paid if the customer were killed.

polygon *noun*
A polygon is a flat **shape** with edges that are **straight lines**. If all the edges are the same **length** and all the **interior angles** are the same **size**, the polygon is called a **regular** polygon.
A square table top is a regular polygon.

polyhedron (plural **polyhedra**) *noun*
A polyhedron is a **solid shape** with many flat **surfaces** called faces. A **dodecahedron**, an **icosahedron**, and a **tetrahedron** are all examples of polyhedra.
They drew a polyhedron with ten faces.

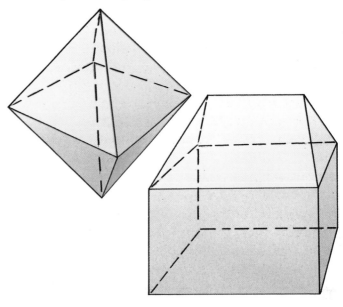

107

polynomial *noun*
A polynomial is a mathematical expression that consists of more than two terms connected by plus signs or minus signs. For example, the expression $2x + 3y - 4z$ is a polynomial. Polynomials are used in the branch of mathematics called **algebra**.
The algebra students learned how to solve equations that contained polynomials.

polyomino *noun*
A polyomino is a flat **shape** made by joining **squares** together. Polyominos have special names, depending on the **number** of squares that are joined. Polyominos can be used in **tessellation**.
The face of the table was a polyomino made of wooden squares.

Name of polyomino	Number of squares
Domino	2
Tromino	3
Tetromino	4
Pentomino	5

portfolio *noun*
A portfolio is a list of **investments** owned by a **company** or an individual. For example, a real estate company may have a large portfolio of houses that it owns.
The value of the shares in the portfolio was $24,000.

positive number *noun*
A positive number is a **number** that is greater than **zero**. **Adding** a positive number to another number always gives a number of higher **value**. For example, 7 is a positive number. If 7 is added to 5 the answer is 12, and 12 has a higher value than either 7 or 5.
The two positive numbers were added together to obtain a second, greater positive number.

possession *noun*
A possession is something that is owned.
His most valuable possession was his condominium.
possess *verb*

post meridiem ▶ P.M.

post office *noun*
A post office is an organization that receives and delivers letters and parcels. It receives payment through sales of postage stamps of various values which must be fixed to the letter or package.
They purchased three first-class stamps from the post office.

pound *noun*
The pound is the **unit** of **currency** of several countries of the world, such as Lebanon, Sudan, and Syria.

pound *noun*
A pound is an **imperial measure** of **weight**. It is written lb in its short form. It is equal to 16 ounces or 453.59 **grams** in **metric** measures.
He bought a pound of sugar.

pound sterling *noun*
The pound sterling is the **currency** of Britain. It is made up of 100 pence.

poverty *noun*
Poverty is the condition of not having enough **money** to **buy** the necessities of life.
The family lived in poverty, without sufficient food or clothing.

power ► page 110

premium *noun*
1. A premium is an amount of **money** that is **paid** for **insurance**. The premium is usually paid regularly, for example, every **month** or every **year**.
His premium was $45 per month.
2. A premium is a **price** greater than the suggested price. A **buyer** may be forced to pay a premium to **purchase goods** that are very scarce or that have a high **value** to someone else.
The car was priced at $15,000 but fetched a $1,000 premium because it was in short supply.

price *noun*
The price of an item is the amount of **money** that must be **paid** to **purchase** it. A price can be altered by a **discount** or a **premium**.
The price of the car was $25,000.

price war *noun*
A price war is a kind of **competition** that occurs when two or more **companies** compete on **price** in order to **sell** similar **goods**. The price war begins when one company lowers its prices below those of its competitor to attract more **customers**. The second company then lowers its prices even further. Customers may benefit from these price cuts, but in the long term, price wars may cause **businesses** to cut back on **production** or to fail.
The oil companies entered a price war which drove down the cost of gasoline.

prime number *noun*
A prime number is a **number** that can be divided only by 1 or by the number itself. For example, 7 is a prime number because its only **factors** are 1 and 7.
Every prime number bigger than 2 is an odd number.

prism *noun*
A prism is a **solid shape**. It has two ends that are **polygons** of the same **size** and shape. Its sides are **parallelograms** or **rectangles**.
A glass prism will separate white light into a rainbow.

triangular prism

private company *noun*
A private company is any company that is not a **public company**. A private company may be small, and owned by just a few **shareholders**. Its shares cannot be bought and sold by the public.
The business is a private company owned by a husband and wife.

probability *noun*
Probability is the likelihood that something will happen. It is the **ratio** between one result and the total number of possibilities. The probability of throwing a 4 with a **die** is 1:6 because a die has six sides, only one of which shows the number four.
The probability of a coin landing to show heads, not tails, is calculated as 1 in 2.

problem *noun*
A problem is a mathematical **puzzle**. The **solution** to a problem is found by using one of the many mathematical rules, or **formulae**.
The problem was solved using the Pythagorean theorem.

power *noun*

A power is the result, or product, of a number multiplied by itself. For example 5^2 is 5 to the power of 2, or 5 × 5 = 25, so 25 is the second power of 5. 5^3 = 5 x 5 x 5 and the product, 125, is the third power of 5.

Exponents are used to show how often the number is to be multiplied.

They figured out that 100 was the second power of 10.

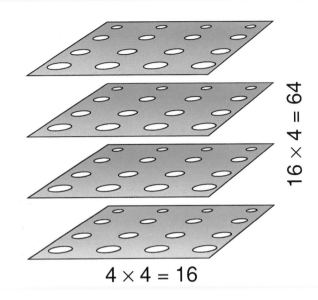

$16 \times 4 = 64$

$4 \times 4 = 16$

4 multiplied by itself 3 times is 4 to the power of 3 and written 4^3. $4 \times 4 \times 4 = 4 \times 4 = 16 \times 4 = 64$.

4 to the power of 1, or 4^1, is 4.

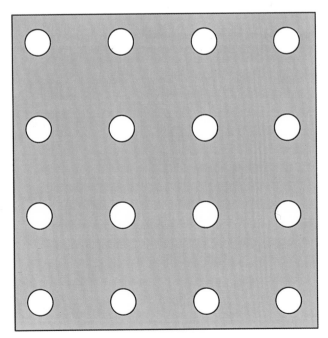

$4 \times 4 = 16$

4^2 is four to the power of 2, or 4×4. The number of 4s in the equation tells you the power.

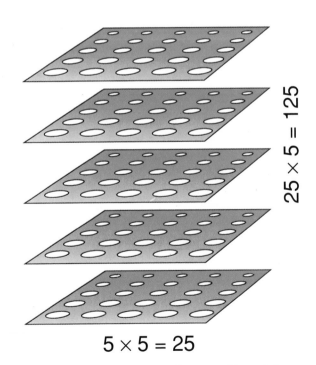

$25 \times 5 = 125$

$5 \times 5 = 25$

5 x 5 x 5 is 5 to the third power or 5^3. If you add up all the dots there are 125.

product *noun*
1. A product is something that a **company** makes or **sells**. The products of a **computer** company are its computers and all the extra pieces of hardware and software that it offers to make the computer work efficiently.
Companies often publish a catalog of their products.
2. A product is the **number** produced when any group of numbers is **multiplied** together. The product of 3 × 4 is 12.
They computed the product of 3 × 5 as 15.

production *noun*
Production is the process of making something. Production can also refer to the **quantity** of things that are made.
The production of cars increased in July.

profit *noun*
A profit is **financial** gain **earned** when the **income** of a **business** is greater than its **expenditures**. A business tries to earn as much income as it can, but it will also have to **pay** out **money** to **buy goods** and other things. If the income it earns is greater than all these **payments**, it makes a profit. The opposite of profit is **loss.**
The company made a profit of $250,000 last year.

profit-and-loss statement *noun*
A profit-and-loss statement is a type of record of **accounts**. It shows how much **net profit** a **business** has made in a given period or how much net loss.
The profit-and-loss statement showed that the company had made a net profit of $100,000 last year.

projection *noun*
1. A projection is a **map** of Earth's surface. Because the Earth's surface is **curved**, when it is drawn on a piece of paper some areas are distorted. Different types of projections try to make up for this inaccuracy.
With a Mercator projection, Earth is drawn as a rectangle.
2. A projection is a kind of **forecast**, or **estimate**, about the future. A **company** will often forecast the **number** of **products** it expects to **sell** in the coming **year**. To do this it will use past information about how many products have been sold in the past.
The sales projection called for 150 videos to be sold this month.

property *noun*
Property is something that is owned by an individual, a group of individuals, or a **company**. It is often used to describe land, but it also refers to all types of **possessions**.
He bought some property near the park.

proportional ▶ **direct proportion**

protractor *noun*
A protractor is an instrument for **measuring angles**. It is usually shaped in the form of a **semicircle**, but a **circular** protractor is useful for measuring **bearings** and certain types of angles. Protractors are marked on the **curved** edge to show the **number** of **degrees** of the angle.
She used the protractor to measure the angles of the triangle.

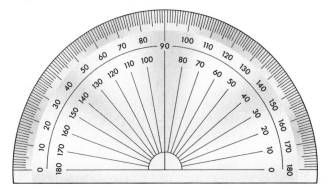

public company   *noun*
A public company is a **company** with **shares** that can be **bought** and **sold** by members of the public, usually on a **stock exchange**. Public companies are usually large and have many **shareholders**.
The public company decided to sell more shares to raise cash for a new factory.

purchase   *verb*
To purchase is to buy.
He purchased a new car.
purchase   *noun*

pure mathematics   *noun*
Pure mathematics describes the study of mathematical problems for their own sake. They are not studied in order to provide solutions that will be put to some practical use. The opposite of pure mathematics is **applied mathematics**.
The college offered a course in pure mathematics.

puzzle   *noun*
A puzzle is a kind of problem. In a jigsaw puzzle the problem is to fit all the pieces together properly.
A math problem is a kind of puzzle.

pyramid   *noun*
A pyramid is a **solid shape**. It has a flat **polygon base**, and its sides rise up to a **point**, or **apex,** at the top. Each of the sides is a **triangle**.
The Egyptians built tombs for their kings in the shape of a pyramid.

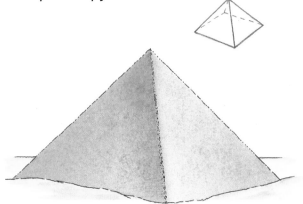

Pythagorean theorem   *noun*
The Pythagorean theorem describes how the **lengths** of the sides of a **right triangle** are related to each other. It states that the **square** of the **hypotenuse** is equal to the square of the other two sides. The Pythagorean theorem is written as $c^2 = a^2 \times b^2$, where c is the length of the hypotenuse and a and b are the lengths of the other two sides. The Pythagorean theorem can be demonstrated by drawing squares on the edges of the triangle. The **area** of the square on the hypotenuse is equal to the **sum** of the areas on the other two sides.
The ancient Egyptians used the Pythagorean theorem when they built the pyramids.

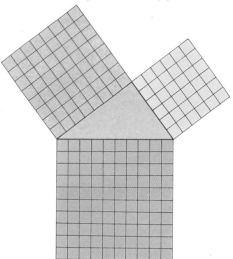

quadrant *noun*
A quadrant is one **quar**ter of a **circle**. The **angle** at the center of a quadrant is always a **right angle**.
The quadrant in the circle was colored red.

quadrilateral *noun*
A quadrilateral is a **polygon** that has four sides. There are many kinds of quadrilateral. **Rectangles**, **parallelograms**, and **rhombuses** are all quadrilaterals.
The angles in a quadrilateral add up to 360°.

quadruple *verb*
To quadruple is to **multiply** any given **number** by four.
The sales figures should quadruple this year.

quality control *noun*
Quality control describes how goods made in a factory are inspected to make sure they are of high standard.
The finished coats passed through quality control.

quantity *noun*
A quantity is an amount. Quantities can be described in **numbers**.
After 250 books were sold in one morning, the quantity of books in the store was decreased.

quart *noun*
A quart is an **imperial measure** of **capacity** equal to two **pints**, or a **quarter** of a **gallon**.
They drank only a quart of orange juice at the party.

quarter *noun*
1. Quarter is one of the parts of something that has been **divided** into four equal parts. It is one fourth of something. A quarter of 20 is 5 because when 20 is **divided** into four equal parts, each part is worth 5. One quarter can also be written $\frac{1}{4}$.
A quarter of 12 is 3.
2. A quarter is a United States coin worth 25 **cents**. It is a quarter of a **dollar**.
The candy bar cost a quarter.

quetzal *noun*
The quetzal is the **currency** of Guatemala. It is made up of 100 centavos.

quipu *noun*
A quipu was a **set** of colored strings with knots. It was used in ancient Peru for **counting** and also as a form of **calendar**.
He counted the amount of gold he had on the quipu.

quotient *noun*
The quotient is the **result** that is obtained when one **number** is **divided** by another.
They quotient of 28 divided by 7 is 4.

113

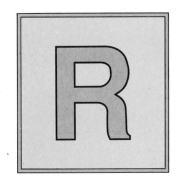

radius (plural **radii**)   *noun*
The radius of a **circle** is the **distance** in a straight line from the center to the edge. This distance is always **half** the length of the **diameter**.
The radius of the circle measured 5 inches.

rand   *noun*
The rand is the **currency** of South Africa. A rand is equal to 100 cents. South Africa also has a specially minted gold coin called a krugerand.

random   *adjective*
Random describes things that happen by **chance**. When things are chosen at random, it means that they are chosen without making a plan or without any particular **pattern**.
The team members were chosen at random, out of a hat.

rate   *noun*
1. Rate refers to how many **units** of one thing occur in something else. Speed is a rate because it **measures** how many **miles** are traveled each **hour**.
The crowd entered the stadium at a rate of 2,000 each hour.
2. Rate is an amount of **money charged** for a **service**. For example, an **accountant** might charge $50 per hour for his or her services. A **bank** might **lend** money and charge an **interest** rate of 10 **percent** per **year**.
The rate of pay for this employee is $10 per hour.

rate of exchange   *noun*
The rate of exchange is the **price** at which one **currency** is exchanged for another. It is usually different, depending on whether a currency is being **bought** or **sold**, and can **vary** according to where the **transaction** takes place. The rate of exchange varies daily as the **value** of one currency moves against another according to **demand**.
The rate of exchange for the British pound in New York was $1.50 on Saturday, but it rose to $1.53 on Monday.

ratio ► page 116

ration   *noun*
A ration is a limited amount of something. For example, if gasoline becomes scarce its distribution may be controlled by the government. Each share is called a ration.
Everyone had to wait in line to receive their ration of bread.
rationing   *noun*
ration   *verb*

rational number   *noun*
A rational number is a **number** that can be written as a **fraction**. For example, 0.625 is a rational number because it can also be written as $\frac{5}{8}$. Rational numbers include all whole numbers because they can be written as a fraction with a **denominator** of 1.
9 is a rational number when it is written as the fraction $\frac{9}{1}$.

real *noun*
A real is a **silver coin** that was once used in Spain and its colonies.

real estate *noun*
Real estate means land and the buildings on it.
The real estate on the coast was worth $25 million.

receipt *noun*
A receipt is a piece of paper that is given to **customers** when they **buy** something. It proves where the item was bought and how much it cost.
When he returned the radio to the store, he had to show the receipt.
receive *verb*

receiver *noun*
A receiver is a person who takes over responsibility for the **property** of a **bankrupt company**.
The bank appointed a receiver to a company with $1 million of debt.

receivership *noun*
Receivership is the condition a **company** is in when its **assets** are under the control of a **receiver**.
The bicycle company went into receivership when its debts became too great to pay.

recession *noun*
A recession is a time when **economic** activity slows down. **Businesses** find that they cannot **sell** as many **goods** as before. As a result, **manufacturing** companies also slow down **production**. Companies need fewer **employees**, and some people are likely to lose their **jobs**.
Many countries have suffered from a recession in recent years.

reciprocal *noun*
The reciprocal of a **number** is 1 **divided** by the number. The reciprocal of 4 is $\frac{1}{4}$. If a number is **multiplied** by its reciprocal the answer is always 1. For example, $4 \times \frac{1}{4} = 1$.
The reciprocal of 5 is $\frac{1}{5}$.

rectangle *noun*
A rectangle is a flat **shape**, or **polygon**, that has four sides, each of which meets another side at a **right angle**. The opposite sides of a rectangle are always equal in **length**.
The pages of a book make a rectangle.

rectangular number *noun*
A rectangular number is a **number** that can be arranged as a rectangular **pattern** of dots. Six is a rectangular number. Seven is not a rectangular number. All **even numbers** above 2 are rectangular numbers.
No prime number can be a rectangular number.

reduce *verb*
To reduce is to make smaller or **less**. Reducing is often used when working out **percentages**.
The store reduced the price of the shirt by 10%.
reduction *noun*

refinance *verb*
Refinance means to get or give a new **loan** for something. A bank might refinance a loan to a company.
When interest rates fell, he decided to save money by refinancing his mortgage.

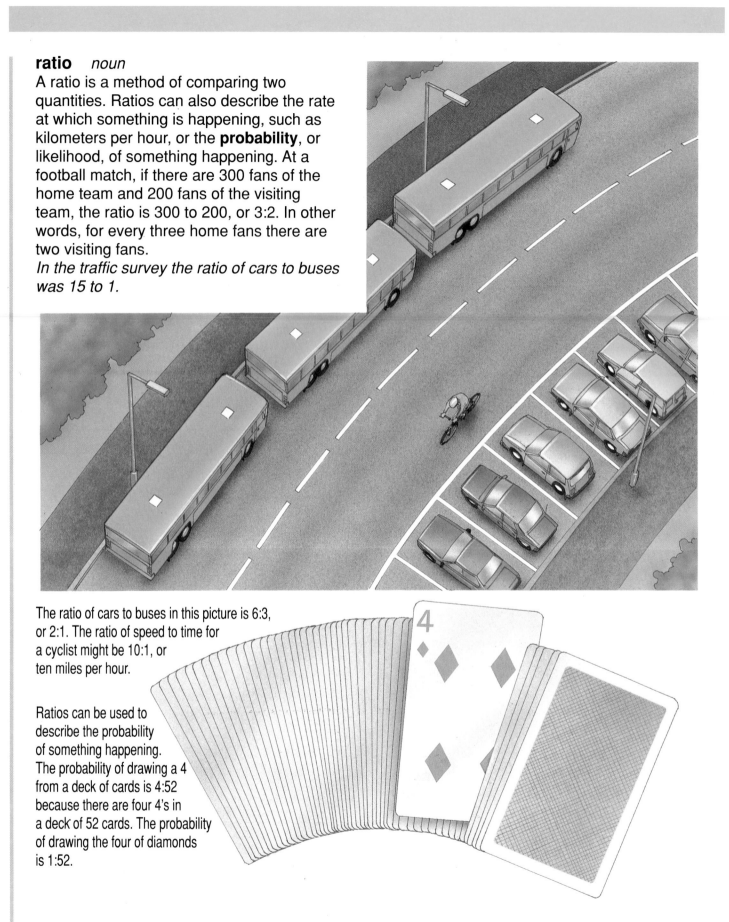

ratio   *noun*

A ratio is a method of comparing two quantities. Ratios can also describe the rate at which something is happening, such as kilometers per hour, or the **probability**, or likelihood, of something happening. At a football match, if there are 300 fans of the home team and 200 fans of the visiting team, the ratio is 300 to 200, or 3:2. In other words, for every three home fans there are two visiting fans.

In the traffic survey the ratio of cars to buses was 15 to 1.

The ratio of cars to buses in this picture is 6:3, or 2:1. The ratio of speed to time for a cyclist might be 10:1, or ten miles per hour.

Ratios can be used to describe the probability of something happening. The probability of drawing a 4 from a deck of cards is 4:52 because there are four 4's in a deck of 52 cards. The probability of drawing the four of diamonds is 1:52.

the golden ratio

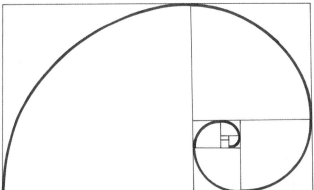

When a square is taken away from a golden rectangle, another golden rectangle is left. This can be repeated many times.

The golden ratio is also known as the golden section or divine proportion. It is approximately 1:1.618. A rectangle the length and width of which match this ratio is very pleasing to the eye, and is called a golden rectangle.

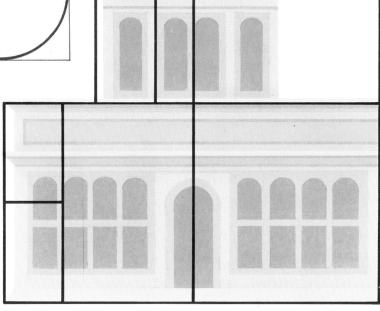

The golden ratio has been applied to many buildings.

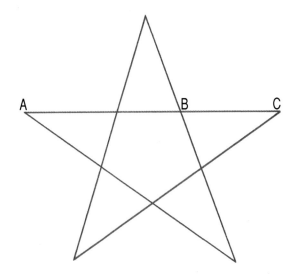

The ratio of AB to BC on a pentagram is the golden ratio.

The golden ratio can often be found in nature.

reflection   *noun*
A reflection is a form of **symmetry**. If a **line** is drawn down the middle of an **isosceles triangle**, the side on the left of the line is a backwards copy, or reflection, of the side on the right. If you looked in a mirror placed down the center, each side and its reflection would look like the whole triangle.
Each side of the playing card is a reflection of the other side.

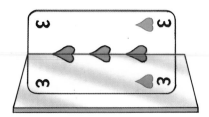

reflex angle   *noun*
A reflex angle is an **angle** that is bigger, or greater, than 180° but smaller, or less, than 360°. At ten minutes to two, the angle between the hour hand and the minute hand is a reflex angle.
When she opened the fan too far, the two arms made a reflex angle.

regular shape   *noun*
A regular shape has sides of equal **length** and **angles** of equal **size**.
A square is a regular shape.

reimburse   *verb*
Reimburse means to pay back an amount of **money** that you owe. For example, a company might reimburse an employee for expenses he or she paid.
He reimbursed her for his share of the bill.

remainder   *noun*
A remainder is any **number** that is left over when one number is **divided** by another. r is the symbol for a remainder.
14 divided by 4 gives an answer of 3 remainder 2.

remuneration   *noun*
Remuneration is a **payment** made to someone for doing a **job**.
His remuneration was $2,000.

Renminbi Yuan   *noun*
The Renminbi Yuan is the **currency** of China. It consists of 10 jiao.

rent   *noun*
Rent is a **payment** made for the use of an asset, often an expensive piece of equipment, a car, or a building. It is paid to the person who owns the asset. Rent is usually paid at regular intervals, usually once a month or year.
Some companies pay rent to use a factory building.
rent   *verb*

repay   *verb*
Repay means to **pay** back **money** that has been **borrowed**.
He had to repay the loan that he had obtained from the bank.
repayment   *noun*

reserve   *noun*
A reserve is an amount of **money** that is set aside until it is needed for some particular purpose.
He had a reserve of a thousand dollars in case of emergency.

result   *noun*
A result is an answer, or outcome, obtained when a **problem** is **solved**.
The result of the equation proved the theory to be true.

retail   ► page 120

retail *verb*
To retail is to **sell** goods to individuals.
The shop retailed cameras and video recorders.

retail price index *noun*
The retail price index is a **number**, or **index**, used to indicate whether the **retail prices** of **goods** sold in **stores** throughout a country are going up or down.
The retail price index showed that prices of stereo equipment had dropped during the year.

revenue ► income

revolution *noun*
A revolution, in mathematics, refers to a full turn of 360°. The **second** hand on a **clock** face turns through one revolution every 60 seconds. Objects and **diagrams** are sometimes revolved in **geometry** to test them on different **coordinates**.
A car wheel makes one revolution every time it spins.

rhombus *noun*
A rhombus is a **parallelogram** that has all its sides of equal **length**. Two of its **opposite angles** are **obtuse angles** and the other two are **acute angles**.
A rhombus is a diamond shape.

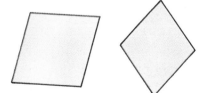

rial *noun*
The rial, sometimes spelled riyal, is the **unit** of **currency** of several Middle Eastern countries, including Iran, Oman, Qatar, and Saudi Arabia.

right angle *noun*
A right angle is an **angle** that measures exactly 90°.
The angles in a square are right angles.

right triangle *noun*
A right triangle is a **triangle** in which one of the **angles** is 90°. The **sum** of the other two angles is always 90°.
The 90° angle in each of these right triangles is identified by a red box.

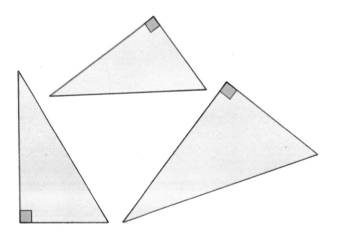

ringgit *noun*
The ringgit is the **currency** of Malaysia. It consists of 100 sen.

risk *noun*
In **business**, risk is the possibility of losing **money**. A **company** might take a risk and **buy** an **expensive** machine to make a new kind of **product**. If the company cannot **sell** enough of the product, the money it **spent** on the machine will be lost. Banks consider risk carefully before lending money.
The directors thought carefully about the risk before they bought the factory.

riyal ► rial

retail *verb*

To retail is to sell to an individual, usually in a store. Retail is different from **wholesale**. Wholesale goods are sold only to other businesses in bulk. Retailing involves everything necessary to operate a store, from waiting on customers to ordering and displaying goods.

The flower shop also retails flowers from a stall in the market.

retail adjective

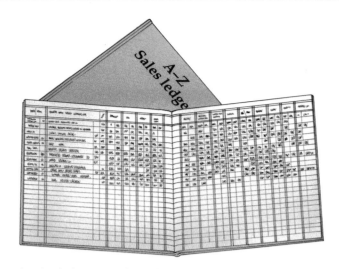

A sales ledger records each transaction. Today, this information is often held on computer.

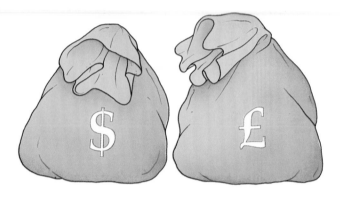

Money comes into the store in payment for goods sold, and is deposited in the bank.

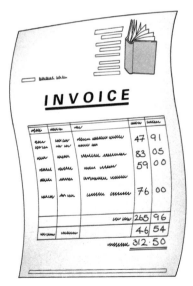

Invoices from suppliers must be paid.

This shop is a retail bookshop.

Advertising on television helps to boost sales.

Books must be ordered and delivered to keep the shelves stocked.

The goods sold by the shop are displayed in the window.

Packaging carrying the bookshop's logo is a kind of advertising.

The bar code on the back of the book gives coded information that can be recorded on computer.

Roman numeral *noun*

Roman numerals are letters that were used as **numerals** by the Romans in ancient times. They were later replaced by **decimal numbers**.

Some clock faces still use Roman numerals to indicate the hours.

Roman number	Decimal number
I	1
II	2
III	3
IV	4
V	5
X	10
L	50
C	100
D	500
M	1000

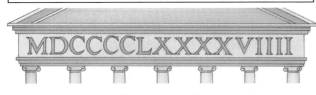

Roman numerals
for 1999

root *noun*

A root is a **number** that is **multiplied** by itself. A **square root** is a number that is multiplied by itself once, and a **cube root** is multiplied by itself twice. Another name for root is **power**.

The fourth root of 16 is 2 because 2 × 2 × 2 × 2 = 16.

rotate *verb*

Rotate is to turn or to move around a central hub or **axis**. **Shapes** are rotated in **geometry** when they are **symmetrical**. To rotate is also to cause something to turn on an axis

Earth rotates on its axis once every 24 hours.

rotation *noun*

rouble ► **ruble**

round *verb*

To round is to change a **number** by increasing it or decreasing it to the nearest ten, hundred or thousand. If the answer to a problem if 2,325, the answer rounded to the nearest hundred is 2,300. A number like 2,372 would be rounded upward to 2,400 because 2,372 is nearer 2,400 than it is to 2,300.

Some decimal fractions need rounding because they continue infinitely.

round number ► round

royalty *noun*

A royalty is a **payment** made to the creator of an invention, book, etc., for its use. A royalty might also be offered to a land owner for the right to dig a mine on his or her land. A royalty normally represents a **percentage** of the **profit** or the **sale price** of an item.

The author received a royalty of seven percent on the sales of his first novel.

ruble *noun*

The ruble was the **currency** of the Soviet Union. It is still the currency of the Russian Republic. There are 100 kopekcs in a ruble.

ruler *noun*

A ruler is a strip of metal, plastic, or wood with a straight edge. It is used when drawing a **straight line** or when **measuring** the **length** of a short object. A ruler is usually marked in **inches** or **centimeters**.

The student used a ruler to draw a straight line between the two points.

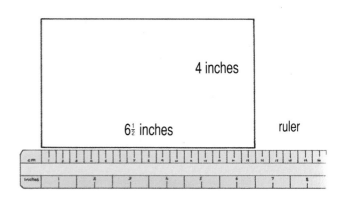

4 inches

$6\frac{1}{2}$ inches

ruler

rupee *noun*
The rupee is the **unit** of **currency** of several countries of the world, including India, Nepal, Pakistan, and Sri Lanka. In India and Pakistan, the rupee is **divided** into 100 paise, and in Nepal, into 100 pice. In Sri Lanka the rupee is equal to 100 cents.

rupiah *noun*
The rupiah is the **currency** of Indonesia. There are 100 sen in one rupiah.

safe ► page 124

safe-deposit box *noun*
A safe-deposit box is usually found in a **bank**. **Customers rent** safe-deposit boxes to store **valuables**, such as **money**, documents, ornaments, or jewelry.
The diamond ring was put in a safe-deposit box at the local bank.

salary *noun*
A salary is a fixed amount of **money** that an **employee** is **paid** to do a **job** for a given period of time. It is usually paid over a **year**. A salary is normally paid to workers in non-manual, or white collar, jobs.
Her salary is $25,000.

sale *noun*
1. A sale is an exchange of **goods** for **money**.
He made a sale of goods worth $3,000.
2. A sale is an offering of a **company**'s **goods** at lower **prices** than usual. **Stores** often do this to clear out old **stock** and make space for new goods.
The department store had a sale during January.

sales tax *noun*
Sales tax is a **tax paid** by **customers** when they **buy goods**. It is usually a **percentage** of the **price** of the goods. It is the government's job to decide on which goods to levy, or charge, sales tax. In many countries some goods, such as books or children's clothes, are not taxed.
The local sales tax was five percent.

safe *noun*

A safe is a fireproof and burglar-proof room, or a strong box that is fastened by a door with a lock on it. Banks use safes to hold money and other valuable items. Safe deposit boxes are located in a special sealed room, or vault. Nobody can go in unless they are accompanied by a bank guard or official.

The bank locked the safe at 5 o'clock.

This type of safe is often found in a branch bank. The door is very thick.

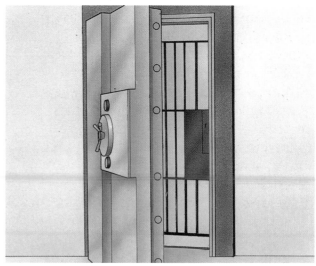

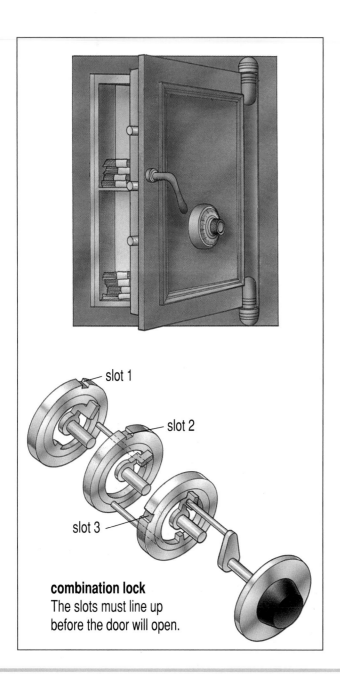

slot 1

slot 2

slot 3

combination lock
The slots must line up before the door will open.

Safe deposit boxes are rented by people who want to protect their valuables. The boxes may be small drawers or larger safes.

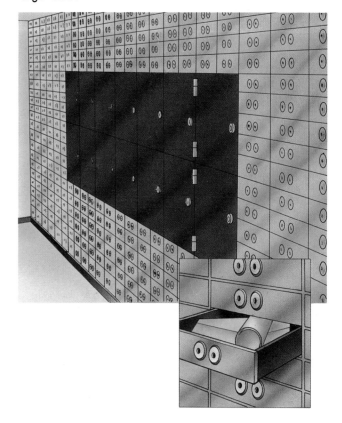

savings   *plural noun*

Savings are amounts of **money** that are kept and not **spent**. People save money when they keep more than they spend. They often **deposit** the money into a **bank**, where it can **earn interest**. They can later **withdraw** the money if they need it.

Her savings amounted to $500.

savings bond   *noun*

A savings bond is a kind of **investment**. **Interest** is **paid** on the **money** used to **buy** the **bond**. After a period of time the bond can be exchanged for the **price** paid plus **interest**.

Savings bonds are issued by the U.S. government.

scalar   *adjective*

Scalar describes a **number** that shows **size** but not direction. Scalar numbers are used to indicate **measurements** like temperature, **volume**, or **time**. All scalar numbers can be **plotted** on a **scale**. They are different from **vectors**.

Scalar numbers were used to show the number of quarts in the pitchers.

scale   *noun*

1. A scale is a **set** of marks on a **line** used for **measuring**. The scale of a **ruler** shows **inches**. The scale of a **protractor** shows **degrees** of **angle**, while the scale of a **thermometer** shows degrees of temperature.

She saw on the thermometer scale that the temperature was 20° Fahrenheit.

2. A scale is a machine used for **weighing**.

The chef weighed the flour on the scale.

3. On a **map** or drawing, a scale shows the **proportion** between the size of the drawings and the size of the actual object. A small **measurement** on paper represents a larger one in real life. For instance, one inch on a map might represent one **mile** across land.

The scale of the map was one inch to one mile.

scalene triangle   *noun*

A scalene triangle is a **triangle** in which all the sides are different **lengths**.

In a scalene triangle each angle is different.

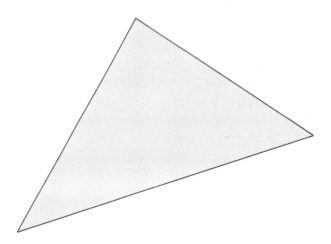

schilling   *noun*

The schilling is the **currency** of Austria. The schilling is made up of 100 groschen.

score   *noun*

A score is a record of points made in a game or on a test either by an individual, or in the case of a game, by each side playing in the game.

The average score on the test was 80 percent.

second   *noun*

1. A second is a **unit** of **time**. There are 60 seconds in a **minute**.

The athlete ran 100 yards in eight seconds.

2. A second is a **unit** of **angle**. There are 60 seconds in a minute of angle.

The angle measured 90 degrees and 30 seconds.

sector   *noun*

A sector is part of a **circle**. It is the **area** between two **radii** and the **circumference** of the circle. A wedge of pie is shaped like a sector. A sector can be used as a numerical indicator in a pie chart when the circle stands for the whole.

They broke the circle into sectors to make a pie chart.

security   *noun*
A security is a **stock**, or **share**.
Their securities included stocks in four different companies.

segment   *noun*
1. A segment is part of a line.
He measured the line segment from A to D.
2. A segment is part of a **circle**. It is the space between a **chord** and the **circumference** of the circle. A **semicircle** is a large segment of a circle.
The circle was divided into two unequal segments.

sell   *verb*
To sell is to **supply goods** or **services** in exchange for **money**.
A bookshop sells books.
seller   *noun*

semicircle   *noun*
A semicircle is a **shape** made by **dividing** a **circle** in **half**.
When the fan was fully opened it made a semicircle.

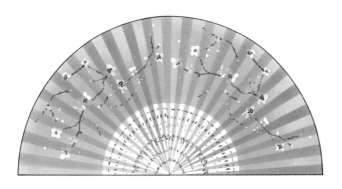

sequence   *noun*
A sequence is a **set** of things arranged in a particular order. The **digits** in the **number** 53864 make a sequence. If this set of digits is arranged in **increasing** order they form a different sequence, 34568. If you recognize the sequence in which a line of numbers is written, you can figure out the next number.
A binary number is a sequence of 0s and 1s.

serial number   *noun*
A serial number is a **number** that is used to identify something. Serial numbers help **companies** keep track of the things they make. A company that makes CD players will give a different serial number to each machine so that the company knows exactly which and how many have been sold. Cars have serial numbers on their chasis to help identify each one.
The police asked the owner to identify his stolen radio by its serial number.

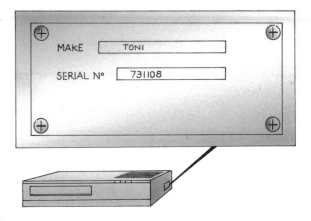

series   *noun*
A series is a **sequence** of **numbers** that follow a **pattern**. For example, in the series 7 11 15 19 it can be seen that the numbers form a pattern because 4 is **added** to each new number. So, the next numbers in the series will be 23 and 27.
They found the pattern in the series by figuring out the difference between each number in it.

services   *plural noun*
Services are **jobs** that people carry out for **customers** or **clients**. For example, an auto mechanic repairs cars, and an **accountant** prepares **accounts** and advises about **taxes**. The government of a country often provides many jobs in the services sector. Service **businesses sell** services rather than **goods**.
The company paid for the services of a lawyer.

set *noun*

A set is any collection of things that have something in common. For instance, a group of apples in a basket would be a set, as would the group of all people with brown eyes. A set of numbers is written inside brackets.
The number six belongs to the set of even numbers.

set square *noun*

A set square is a triangle made out of wood or plastic for use in **geometry**. One of the angles of a set square is always a **right angle**.
Draughtsmen use set squares as a guide to drawing lines at angles.

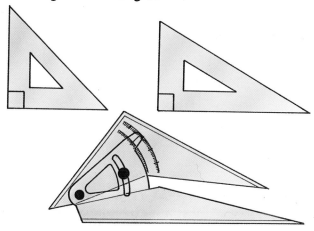

shape (two-dimensional) ► page 128

shape (three-dimensional) ► page 130

share *noun*

A share is a part of the **capital** of a **company**. In order to raise **money**, a company might sell shares. The people who **buy** the shares, called **shareholders**, will then own part of the company. Those with shares can vote on what the company should do, and if the company is successful, they will receive some of its **profits**. Shares are bought and **sold** on a **stock exchange**.
They paid $30 for each share.

shareholder *noun*

A shareholder is someone who owns **shares** in a **company**.
The company paid a dividend to its shareholders last year.

share price *noun*

The share price is the **price** of a **share** in a particular company.
The share price of the company is $1.35.

shekel *noun*

The shekel is the **currency** of Israel.

shop *noun*

A shop is a small **store**. It is a small **retail** business that offers only a limited variety of goods. Many shops specialize in a particular kind of merchandise.
She bought a television at the shop.

significant figures *plural noun*

Significant figures are the **digits** that you keep after **rounding**. If 23.45886 is rounded to four significant figures, only the first four digits are kept, so the answer will be 23.46. The last, or fourth, digit, is rounded upward from 5 to 6.
The value of pi is 3.1416, to five significant figures.

signs and symbols ► page 133

127

shape (two-dimensional)   *noun*

A shape is any form. A two-dimensional shape is the outline of a flat surface. These shapes are also called **plane figures**. If they have straight sides they belong to the group of shapes called **polygons**.

Circles, squares and triangles are all two-dimensional shapes.

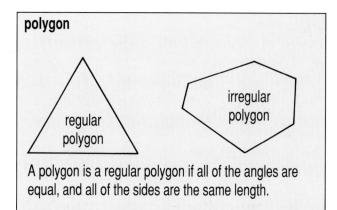

polygon

A polygon is a regular polygon if all of the angles are equal, and all of the sides are the same length.

triangles
Triangles are 3-sided figures.

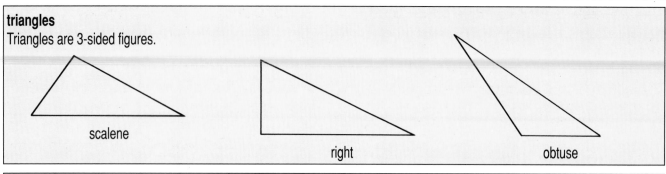

scalene

right

obtuse

quadrilaterals
Quadrilaterals are 4-sided figures.

parallelograms

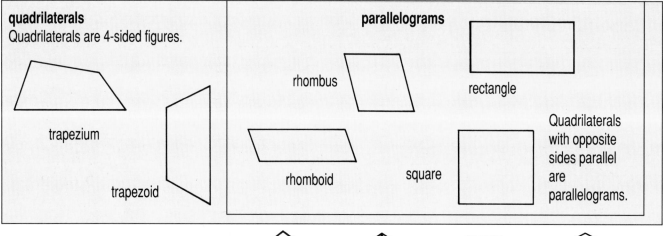

trapezium

trapezoid

rhombus

rhomboid

square

rectangle

Quadrilaterals with opposite sides parallel are parallelograms.

In theory, there is an infinite number of polygons, each with one more side than the last. Not all of these have been named.

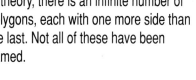

pentagon
5 sides

pentagram
5-sided star

hexagon
6 sides

heptagon
7 sides

octagon
8 sides

nonagon
9 sides

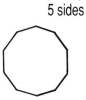

decagon
10 sides

hendecagon
11 sides

dodecagon
12 sides

A circle is a polygon with an infinite number of sides

curves

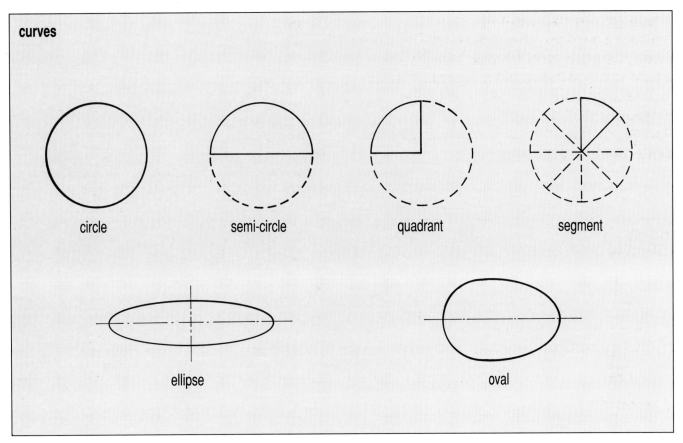

circle

semi-circle

quadrant

segment

ellipse

oval

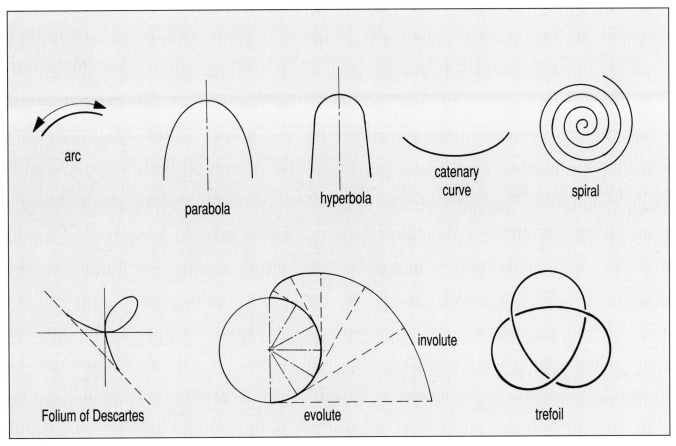

arc

parabola

hyperbola

catenary curve

spiral

Folium of Descartes

evolute

involute

trefoil

shape (three-dimensional)   *noun*

A shape is any form. A three-dimensional shape is also known as a **solid**. Each side of a solid is called a face. If the faces are flat, the shape belongs to a group called **polyhedrons**.

Spheres, cuboids and pentahedrons are all three-dimensional shapes.

tetrahedron
4 faces

pentahedron
5 faces

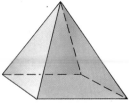

polyhedron

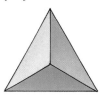

regular polyhedron

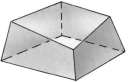

irregular polyhedron

A polyhedron is a three-dimensional solid with flat faces. If all of the faces are exactly the same, it is a regular polyhedron. There are only five regular solids, tetrahedrons, cubes, octahedrons, dodecahedrons and icosahedrons.

hexahedrons

Hexahedrons have 6 faces.

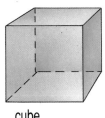

cube

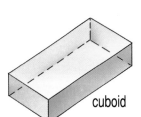

cuboid

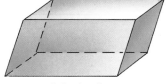

parallelepiped

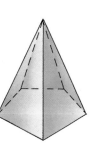

hexagonal pyramid

heptahedron
7 faces

octahedron
8 faces

decahedron
10 faces

dodecahedron
12 faces

icosahedron
20 faces

prisms

Prisms have two parallel faces which are polygons. All the other faces are parallelograms.

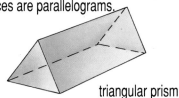

triangular prism

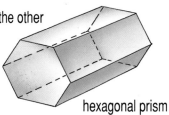

hexagonal prism

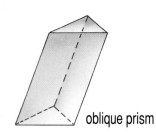

oblique prism

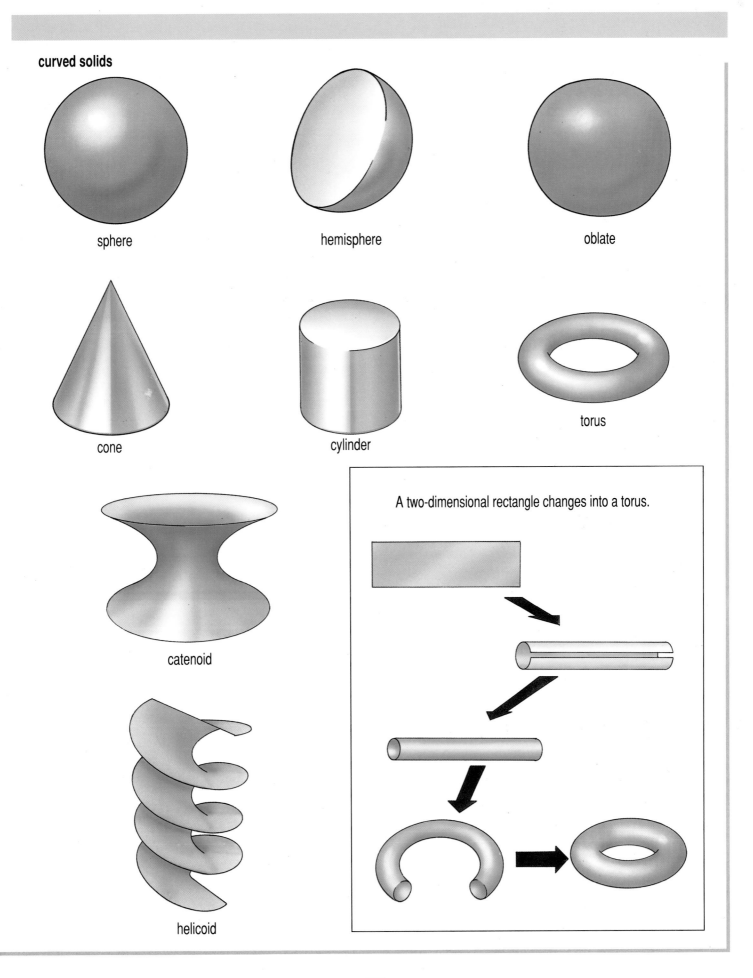

curved solids

sphere

hemisphere

oblate

cone

cylinder

torus

catenoid

helicoid

A two-dimensional rectangle changes into a torus.

silver *noun*
Silver is a valuable metal. It is dug out of the ground at a silver mine. Silver was once used to make **coins**, but now most coins are made of other metals. Silver is used mostly in the manufacture of jewelry.
She bought a necklace made of silver.

similar *adjective*
In **geometry**, similar describes things that are the same **shape** but different **sizes**.
If two triangles are similar, the larger can be reduced to the size of the smaller one.

simple interest *noun*
Simple interest is **interest** that is **calculated** only on the amount of the original **loan**, not on the resulting interest as well.
Simple interest is lower than compound interest.

simplify *verb*
To simplify is to write in a shorter form. A **sequence** of **numbers** in a **problem** can be simplified in order to **solve** it more easily. For example, 3 + (5 + 1) can be simplified to 3 + 6.
It was necessary to simplify the number sequence to arrive at a single digit.

simultaneous equations *plural noun*
Simultaneous equations are two or more **equations** containing more than one unknown quantity. They can be solved by drawing them on a **graph** or by adding the equations together to eliminate one unknown by using substitution.
They solved the problem using simultaneous equations and a graph.

sine *noun*
The sine is the **length** of the side of a **right triangle** that falls opposite an **acute angle**, **divided** by the length of the **hypotenuse**. It is one of the three main **functions** in **trigonometry**.
They measured the sides of the right triangle to find the sine.

Singapore dollar *noun*
The Singapore dollar is the **currency** of Singapore. It is made up of 100 cents.

SI unit *noun*
Système International d'Unité is the International System of Units. It is used by many countries to enable them to compare scientific **results**. The most common SI units are the three bax units. The SI unit of **length** is the **meter**, the SI units of **mass** is the **kilogram**, and the SI unit of **time** is the **second**.
They used SI units to weigh the cartons.

size *noun*
Size is how big something is.
A solid object needs three dimensions to describe its size.

slide rule *noun*
A slide rule is a kind of manual **calculator** designed to work out mathematical **problems**. It resembles a **ruler** with a sliding section in the middle. **Scales** marked on each section must be lined up properly to provide the answer to a problem. The answer is read from one of the scales when it lines up with a line on the sliding section, or cursor.
Slide rules have now been replaced by electronic calculators.

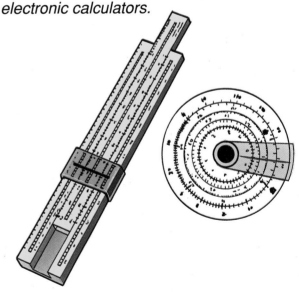

signs and symbols   *plural noun*

Signs and symbols are marks that stand for something else. They often take the place of words, and are quicker to write. Each sign or symbol has a special meaning, but sometimes they have more than one meaning. For example 12' can mean 12 feet or 12 minutes.

Signs and symbols are common in mathematical equations.

Business and commerce

$	dollar
¢	cent
£	pounds sterling
a/c	account
@	at
©	copyright
®	registered trademark

Many mathematical signs and symbols are also used in business and commerce.

Mathematics

+	plus or positive
−	minus or negative
x	multiplied by
•	multiplied by
÷	divided by
=	equal to
≈	approximately equal to
≡	equivalent to
≅	congruent or approximately equal to
≠	not equal to
<	less than
>	greater than
≤	less than or equal to
≥	greater than or equal to
∞	infinity
⊥	perpendicular to
‖	parallel to
:	ratio sign
±	plus or minus
°	degree
'	minute
"	second or seconds
'	foot or feet
"	inch or inches
∴	therefore
π	pi
√	square root

The equal sign is used in equations.

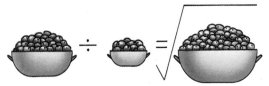

This equation uses division, equal to, and square-root signs.

$$A \perp B$$

A is perpendicular to B.

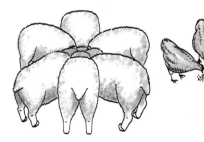

The ratio sign is used to compare two quantities. Six sheep to four chickens is written 6:4.

The ® symbol shows that a trademark has been registered.

slope *noun*
The slope of a **surface** describes the **angle** at which it drops away from a level surface. The slope of a hill is worked out by **measuring** the **height** of the angle compared with the **distance** traveled. If you rise one foot for every four feet you move, the slope is $\frac{1}{4}$, sometimes written as 1 in 4, or 25 **percent**. The slope of a level surface is **zero**. Gradient is another word for slope.
The car could not drive up a slope of 40 percent.

slump *noun*
A slump is a drop in **business** activity. When the economy of a country declines, there is less **money** available to spend so people buy less. The value of things may then decline causing a slump in the **market**.
He lost his job during the slump.

social security *noun*
Social security is a **fund** of **money** raised by the government and used to make **payments** to people who are retired or disabled. The money is raised from **taxes** paid by **employees** and **employers**.
After he was disabled in the mine accident, he was eligible to receive social security payments.

solid *noun*
A solid is a **three-dimensional** object that has **length**, width, and **height**. Most solid **shapes** can be described as **polyhedra**.
A cube is a solid.
solid *adjective*

solution *noun*
A solution is the answer to a problem or question. For example in the equation $3 = x + 1$ the solution is 2. It is written as $x = 2$.
The solution of the equation $4 = x + 7$ is $x = -3$.
solve *verb*

solvency *noun*
Solvency is the ability of a person or a **company** to pay its **debts**. When a company is making more money than it is spending on producing its **goods**, it is in a state of solvency. A company is not allowed to operate if it is not solvent. The opposite of solvency is **insolvency**.
Because of its solvency the company was able to pay the huge shipping bill.
solvent *adjective*

souk *noun*
A souk is a kind of **market** often found in the Middle East and North Africa. It usually has stalls where different sorts of foods and **goods** are sold.
The tourist bought a gold necklace at the souk in Fez.

spend *verb*
To spend is to **pay** out **money** in exchange for **goods** or **services**.
She spent $200 on her new camera.

spendthrift *noun*
A spendthrift is someone who **spends money** carelessly and does not try to save it. The opposite of a spendthrift is a **miser**.
She was a spendthrift because she spent all her allowance on clothes as soon as she received it.

sphere *noun*
A sphere is a perfectly round **solid shape**. If a sphere is cut in two, the outline of the flat **base** is a **circle**. A ball is a sphere.
They built a satellite in the shape of a sphere.

spiral *noun*

A spiral is a type of **curve** that winds around a fixed **point**, steadily moving away from it.
The paper streamer was shaped like a spiral.

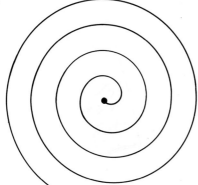

spreadsheet *noun*

A spreadsheet is a sheet of paper with written or printed data on it. It is used by **accountants** and computer operators to help **analyze** data more easily. Computer programs called spreadsheets organize **data** into columns and rows and make **calculations**.
The company accountant used a spreadsheet to compare the sales data on various products.

square *noun*

1. A square is a **rectangle** that has four equal sides. The **angles** of a square are **right angles**.
The lawn was shaped like a square.
2. The square of a **number** is the number **multiplied** by itself. The square of 3 is 3 × 3 = 9. The square of 3 is written 3².
The square of 5 is 25.

square measure *noun*

Square measures are **measurements** of **area**. For example, one square inch measures 1" × 1" and one square yard measures 36" × 36". The area of a football ground is worked out in square yards, or y².
The different fields were compared in size using square measures.

square root *noun*

A square root is a **number** that makes a **square**. The square root of 25 is 5, because the square of 5 is 5 × 5 = 25. A square root can also be described as the **power** of 2.
He worked out the square root of 81 on his calculator.

stake *noun*

A stake is a **sum** of **money**, or something of value, that is put at risk. Usually it is held for the winner of a contest or game.
The stake that he played cards for was $1,000.
stake *verb*

standard *noun*

1. A standard is something that is established to **measure capacity**, **weight**, **distance**, **value**, etc. A **pound**, for example, is a standard of weight, since the weight of objects are compared to the pound.
The mile is a standard of distance.
2. A standard is the basis of value for a **currency**. If a currency uses the **gold standard**, the currency is worth a certain amount of **gold**.
The United States used to use the gold standard.

standard of living *noun*

The standard of living is the **economic** level at which the people of a country live. In a wealthy country, where there is plenty of **money** to **spend** and people **buy** more, the standard of living is said to be high. In poor countries, where **wages** are low and people cannot spend much, the standard of living is said to be low.
The standard of living in the country rose as it became richer from its oil revenues.

star *noun*

A star is a flat **shape** that has sharp **points**. Stars can have any **number** of points, but usually they have five or six.
A star that has five points is a pentagram.

statement *noun*

A statement is a summary of an **account**. It is usually issued monthly or quarterly. It may tell how much **money** a person or a **company** has, or how much is owed.
The statement showed that the company owed the builders $100,000.

statistician *noun*

A statistician is a person who is an expert in **statistics**, or one who keeps statistics. The government and certain types of companies hire statisticians to help them collect and analyze **data**.
He was the statistician for his school football team.

statistics *plural noun*

Statistics are **data** based on **numbers**. Statistics can be used to **forecast** how many people might **buy** a particular kind of **product**, or which party might get the most votes during an election. Usually, the information is collected by researchers. Statistics is also the science of collecting and using facts.
The statistics showed that 30 percent of people prefer to travel by bus.

sterling *noun*

Sterling is short for **pounds sterling**, the **currency** of Britain.

stock *noun*

1. Stock is the **goods** bought or made by a **business** to **sell** to its **customers**, or to use in making other goods. The toys in a shop are its stock. Stock is also called **inventory**.
The stock of the department store was valued at $500,000.
2. Stock is a kind of **investment** in a **company**. The company sells **shares** to **investors**, who become partial owners of the business. Stocks are sometimes called shares.
The stockbroker tried to sell the company's stock for a big profit.
stock *verb*

stockbroker *noun*

A stockbroker is a person whose **job** it is to **buy** and **sell stock**, or **shares**, on behalf of **clients**. A stockbroker often works for a brokerage house.
The careful stockbroker recommended safe stocks to his clients.

stock exchange *noun*

A stock exchange is a place where **stocks**, or **shares**, are **bought** and **sold**. The New York Stock Exchange is the largest stock exchange in the United States.
Stockbrokers buy and sell shares on the stock exchange for their customers.

stock market *noun*

Stock market is another term for **stock exchange** and the **business** conducted there.
The stock market improved as several companies showed huge year end profits.

store *noun*

A store is a place where **customers** are able to **buy goods** at **retail** prices. Many stores stock a wide range of goods.
He bought a newspaper at the store.

straight angle *noun*

A straight angle is an **angle** that **measures** exactly 180°.
The two arms of the fan made a straight angle when the fan was fully opened.

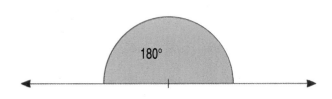

straight line *noun*

A straight line is a **line** that has no bends in it. Straight lines can be drawn with a **ruler**.
He drew a straight line 20 inches long.

strategy *noun*
A strategy is a plan. **Companies** often work out a strategy for **selling** their **goods** in a particular **market**.
The company's sales strategy led to increased sales in California.

strike *noun*
A strike is the refusal of **employees** to work. Usually, they do this to put pressure on their **employer** to make some change.
Employees may strike to get better working conditions or because they feel they are poorly **paid**.
The workers went out on strike for higher wages.
strike *verb*

subset *noun*
A subset is a **set** that is part of a larger set. In a set of pencils of different colors, the pencils can be grouped into subsets of the same color.
The set of blue pencils is a subset of the set of all the pencils.

subsidiary *noun*
A subsidiary is a **company** that is controlled by another company.
Subsidiaries are sometimes created to market new products.

subsidy *noun*
1. A subsidy is a **sum** of **money** paid to **companies** that need **financial** help to stay in **business**. For example, the government of a country might pay a subsidy to the automobile **industry** so that it can **sell** cars at a **price competitive** with **imports**.
The farmers received a large government subsidy.
2. A subsidy is a sum of money paid to **finance** a nonprofit organization. For example, a government might **pay** a subsidy to a hospital so it can provide medical services.
Many schools have received government subsidies in the past.

substitute *verb*
To substitute is to replace one thing with another in an **equation**. If 2 is substituted for x in the equation $3 = x + 1$, the equation becomes $3 = 2 + 1$. Both sides of this new equation are equal, so the **solution** of the equation is $x = 2$.
This equation was solved by substituting 2 for x.
substitution *noun*

subtract *verb*
To subtract is to take away. In an **equation**, subtraction is represented by a **minus sign** $(-)$. $10 - 8 = 2$ is a subtraction **problem**.
He had to subtract four cakes from the ten he had, and he was left with six.
subtraction *noun*

sum *noun*
The sum of two **numbers** is the total when the numbers are **added** together.
The sum of 4 and 5 is 9.

supermarket *noun*
A supermarket is a large **store** that **sells** groceries and other household **goods**. **Customers** help themselves to the goods they want from the shelves, placing them in a basket or cart. The goods are **paid** for at the checkout.
She did all her week's shopping at the supermarket that was just around the corner.

137

survey *verb*

1. To survey is to examine a subject by asking questions. Businesses often carry out a survey to find out who and where their customers are, and what they want to buy.
The company plans to survey book-buying habits in the city.

2. To survey is to measure and map a certain area. A survey includes details of the boundary, elevation and position of the things in the area. **Geometry** and **trigonometry** are used in making the measurements.
A local company was hired to survey the building site.

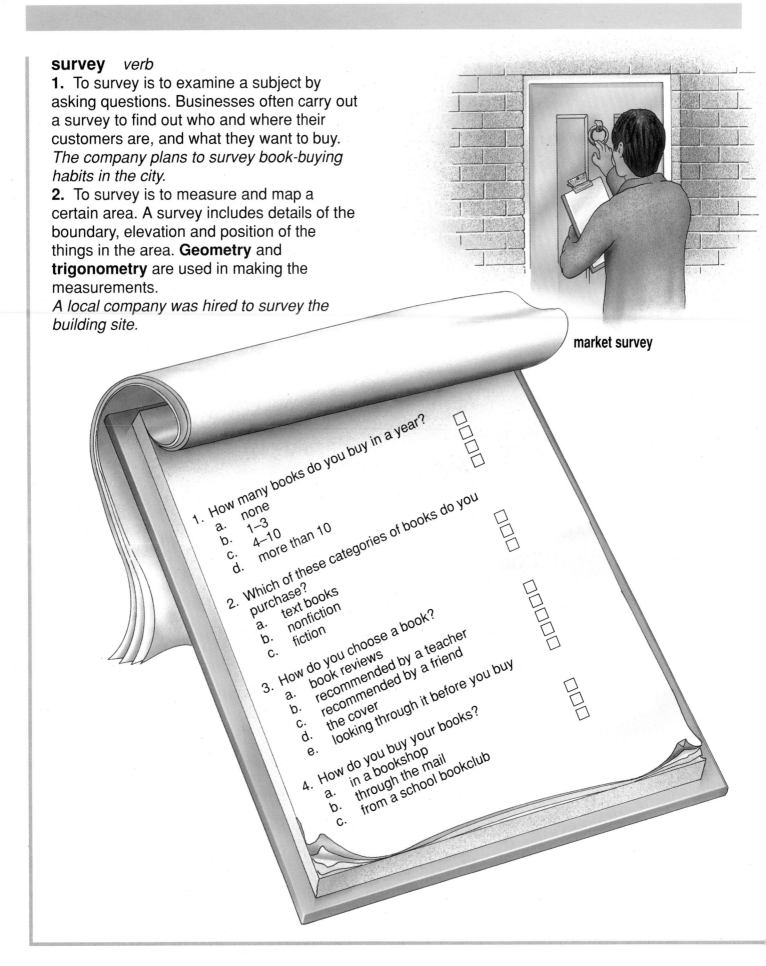

market survey

1. How many books do you buy in a year?
   a. none
   b. 1–3
   c. 4–10
   d. more than 10

2. Which of these categories of books do you purchase?
   a. text books
   b. nonfiction
   c. fiction

3. How do you choose a book?
   a. book reviews
   b. recommended by a teacher
   c. recommended by a friend
   d. the cover
   e. looking through it before you buy

4. How do you buy your books?
   a. in a bookshop
   b. through the mail
   c. from a school bookclub

land survey

tape survey

The distance between A and B can be measured by stretching a steel tape horizontally between the two points.

tacheometry (stadia) survey

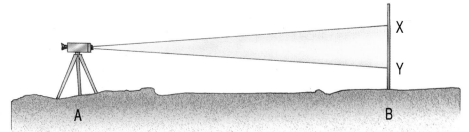

The distance between the instrument A and the staff B can be calculated by the difference between the two stadia readings, X and Y.

EDM survey

An EDM (electronic distance measurement) instrument at point A sends a signal to a target at point B. It then calculates the distance, according to how long it takes for the signal to travel.

leveling

Leveling is a method of measuring the difference in height between points. The surveyor looks through an instrument called a level at a measuring stick called a staff. A measurement is taken of the height showing on the staff at point A. Then the staff is moved to point B, the level swung around, and another measurement is taken. The surveyor can then calculate the height of the instrument and the height of point B.

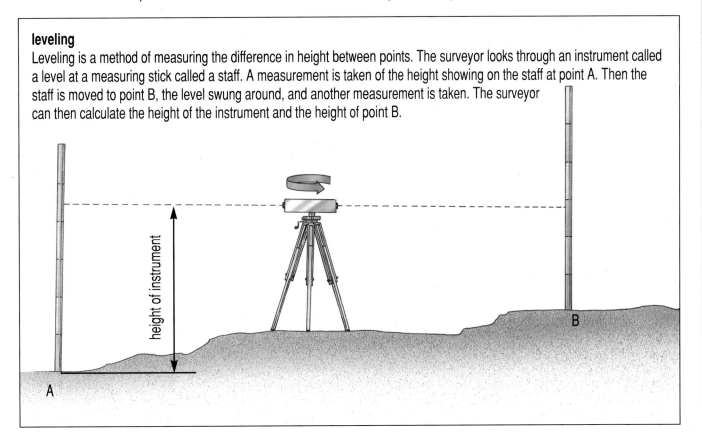

supplementary angles   *plural noun*
Supplementary angles are **angles** that **add** up to 180°.
60° and 120° are supplementary angles.

supplier   *noun*
A supplier is a person or a **company** that **sells goods** or **services** to **customers**.
The supplier delivered the fresh fruit to the supermarket each day.

supply   *verb*
To supply is to provide **goods** or **services** to **customers**.
The company said it would supply the supermarket with fresh fruit each day.

supply   *noun*
A supply is a **quantity** of **goods** available for **customers** to **buy**.
A supply of fresh fruit was delivered to the supermarket each day.

supply and demand   *plural noun*
Supply and demand are the two factors that determine the **price** of **goods** in the marketplace. **Supply** is how much of an item is available. **Demand** is how much of an item people want and can afford.
Supply and demand determined the price of the new cars.

surface   *noun*
A surface is the outer face of an object. The surface of a **cube** is made up of six **square** faces.
The surface of the desk is covered with paper.

surplus   *noun*
Surplus is the **money** left over from a **sum** after **payments** for **expenses** have been made. Surplus money is often **profit**.
The charity made a surplus of $240 on the sale of flags.

survey ► page 138

Swiss franc   *noun*
The Swiss franc is the **currency** of Switzerland. A franc is made up of 100 centimes.

symbol   *noun*
A symbol is a sign that stands for something else. For example, the symbol for **degree** is the sign ° and the symbol for **dollars** is $. Symbols are used to represent unknown **numbers** in **algebra**.
We all recognize the symbol ÷.

symmetry ► page 141

syndicate   *noun*
A syndicate is a group of people or **companies**. It is often formed when several companies join together in order to **buy** something too **expensive** for the individual company to buy alone.
The companies formed a syndicate to build the new communications system.

symmetry *noun*

Symmetry means the same on both sides. A rectangle has symmetry because a line drawn down the center creates two identical sides. A circle has symmetry because the hemispheres on either side of the **diameter** match. The line that can be drawn to divide the object is the **axis** of symmetry.

A line of symmetry can be drawn down the center of a butterfly's body.

symmetrical *adjective*

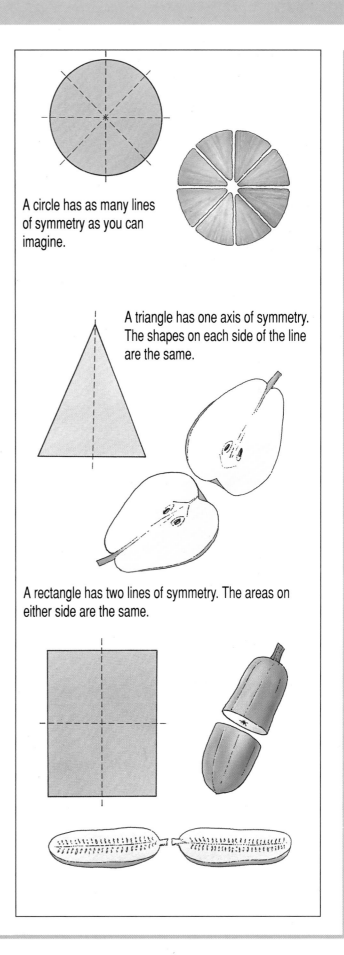

A circle has as many lines of symmetry as you can imagine.

A triangle has one axis of symmetry. The shapes on each side of the line are the same.

A rectangle has two lines of symmetry. The areas on either side are the same.

If a line were drawn through the middle of the Eiffel Tower from top to bottom, both sides of the line would show symmetry.

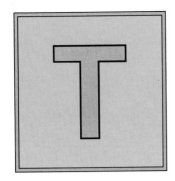

table   *noun*
A table is a list made up of rows and columns of information. Some tables of **numbers** are used for working out **problems**. A railroad **timetable** shows the **time** and destination of each train from a station.
The clerk gave them a table of prices.

talent   *noun*
A talent was a **unit** of **weight** and of **money** used in several countries in ancient times.

tangent   *noun*
1. The tangent of an **angle** in a **right triangle** is the **ratio** produced when the **length** of the side opposite the angle is **divided** by the length of the side **adjacent** to the angle.
The tangent of the triangle was 3:5.
2. A tangent is a **straight line** that just touches a **curve** but does not cross it.
The hammer flew off at a tangent when the thrower let go.

tangram   ►   page 143

tariff   *noun*
A tariff is a **tax** that is **paid** when **goods** are **exported** or **imported**. For example, a government might want people to **buy** cars that are made in their own country. It could place a tariff on imported cars so that they became more **expensive** than the country's own cars.
The government put a tariff on imported washing machines.

tax   *noun*
Tax is **money paid** by people and **companies** to the government.
The amount of **income tax** that people pay depends on how much **income** they earn. The amount of tax that a company pays depends on how much **profit** it makes. The government also raises money from **sales tax**. The government uses taxes to provide **services**, such as hospitals and schools.
The company paid a tax of $1,000.
tax   *verb*

taxable   *adjective*
Taxable describes something that can be taxed by the government. An imported car is taxable as is a part of many people's incomes.
His taxable income was just $5,000.

taxation   *noun*
Taxation is the act of a government of **charging taxes**. It also means the **revenue**, or **money** raised from taxes.
Without taxation the government could not build roads.

taxpayer   *noun*
A taxpayer is a person who **pays tax**. Not all people are taxpayers. You must be earning a specified amount of money before the government charges tax. Unemployed people cannot be taxpayers.
The taxpayer asked his accountant to work out his tax bill.

tangram *noun*
A tangram is an ancient Chinese puzzle consisting of a square cut into seven pieces. These are five triangles, a square and a **parallelogram**. The seven pieces can be combined to form many different figures and shapes.
She made a bird with the tangram.

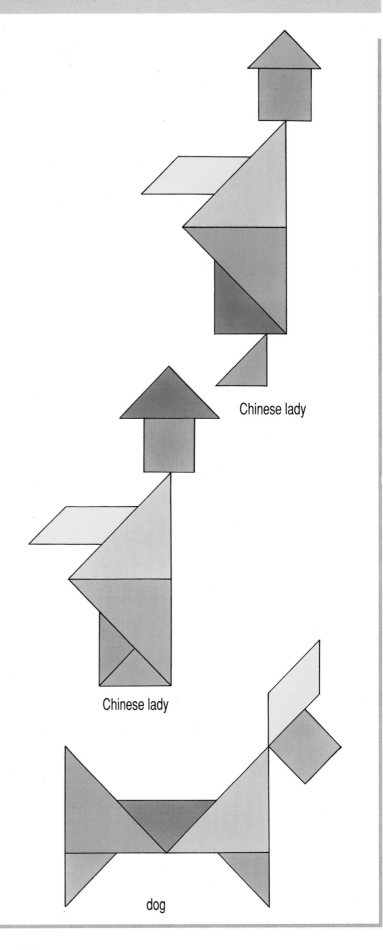

Chinese lady

Chinese lady

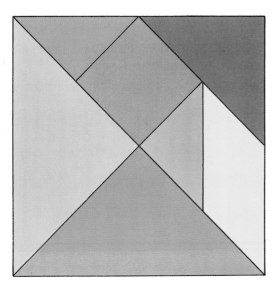

The rectangle is divided into different shapes. All the triangles are equilateral.

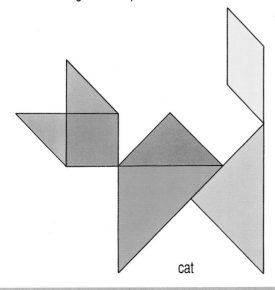

cat

dog

telecommunications *plural noun*
Telecommunications are all the methods of communicating over long **distances**. This is made possible by modern information technology, such as **communications** satellites, telephone lines, and messages sent by computer.
The telecommunications network made it possible for him to speak to his friend in New York.

temperature *noun*
Temperature is a **measurement** of how hot or cold something is.
The chef checked the temperature of the oven by looking at the thermometer.

ten *noun*
Ten is the number between 9 and 11. Our number system, the **decimal** system, uses **base** 10.
In base 10, we use the digits 0, 1, 2, 3, 4, 5, 6, 7, 8, and 9.

tenant *noun*
A tenant is an individual or **company** that occupies a building that belongs to someone else, called the **landlord**. A tenant pays **rent** to the landlord.
The tenant paid rent of $200 per month.

tender *verb*
To tender is to offer **money** for something.
He tendered his bus fare.

tender *verb*
A tender is a formal offer of **money** for something. A tender is also an offer to buy a certain amount of a **company's stock** at a certain price. Finally, tender may refer to money offered in payment for something.
Money is sometimes referred to as "legal tender".

tender *noun*
A tender is an offer, usually made in writing, to a **business** or public office, to carry out work or supply **goods** at a fixed **price** or a certain rate over a given period of **time**. The particulars of the job are usually written down by the business or public office.
The construction company tendered for the contract to build a new road.

tessellation ▶ page 146

tetrahedron *noun*
A tetrahedron is a **solid shape** that has four faces. Each face is a **triangle**.
A tetrahedron is a type of polyhedron.

theft *noun*
Theft is the taking of something without the owner's permission. Theft is a crime. Theft applies to ideas, such as the design for a new car, as well as objects.
The man was sentenced to five years in prison for theft.

three-dimensional *adjective*
Three-dimensional describes objects that are **solids**. Three **coordinates** are needed to locate a particular **point** on a three-dimensional object. These refer to **height**, **length**, and width.
A brick is a three-dimensional object.

time *noun*
Time is a way of **measuring** when an event happens and how long it lasts. A **clock** is used to measure time in **seconds**, **minutes**, and **hours**.
A year is also a measure of time.

timetable *noun*
A timetable is a **table** of **figures** that shows when events are due to happen. A railroad timetable shows when each train is due to leave or arrive at a station.
A school timetable shows when each class is due to begin and what the subject will be.

time zone ► page 148

tithe *noun*
A tithe is a tenth. Originally it was a **tax** paid by people who worked on the land. They had to **pay** a tenth of their **produce** or **income** to the landowner.
The family contributed a tithe to their church.

token *noun*
A token is an object that stands for something else. For example, a token can be a small disk that is used instead of **money**.
He paid for the bus ride with a token.

ton *noun*
A ton is an **imperial measure** of **weight**. One ton is equal to 2,000 **pounds** and is equivalent to approximately the **metric** weight of about 907 kilograms.
The factory buys coal by the ton.

tonne *noun*
A tonne is a **metric measure** of **weight**.
One tonne is equal to 1,000 kilograms.

trade *verb*
To trade is to **buy** and **sell**. Trade can also mean to exchange, or **barter**, something that you have for something of about equal **value** that belongs to another person.
He traded a video cassette for a compact disc.

trade *noun*
Trade is the **buying** and **selling** of **goods**. It can also mean **barter**.
The exchange rate affects international trade.

trademark *noun*
A trademark is a **symbol**, a word, or a phrase that a **company** uses to identify its **products**. Sometimes companies create a visual image, called a **logo**, to serve as a trademark.
The trademark of the airline was a picture of a bird in flight.

trader *noun*
A trader is an individual or **company** that **buys** and **sells goods**.
She was a trader in gold.
trade *verb*

transaction *noun*
A transaction is any item of activity carried out by a **business**. For example, **selling** a **product** to a **customer**, **paying wages** to an **employee**, and **depositing money** in a **bank account**, are all transactions.
The transactions of a business are recorded in its books of account.

trapezoid *noun*
A trapezoid is a type of **polygon**, or flat figure with sides that are straight lines. A trapezoid has four sides, only two of which are parallel.
A trapezoid looks like a rectangle with two slanted sides.

trapezium *noun*
A trapezium is a **quadrilateral** in which neither of the pairs of opposite sides is **parallel**.
The lawn was laid out in the shape of a trapezium.

tessellation *noun*

Tessellation is the covering of a flat surface with shapes that fit together exactly.
Equilateral triangles and **regular hexagons** can cover a surface without leaving any gaps.
John made a tessellation out of dominos.

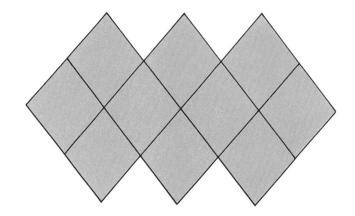

A tessellation using diamonds

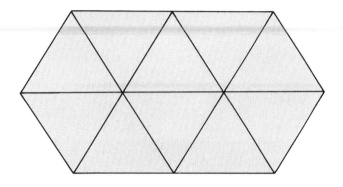

A tessellation using triangles

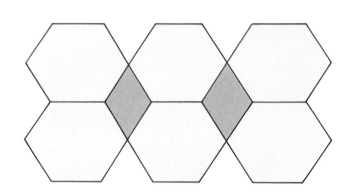

A tessellation using diamonds and hexagons

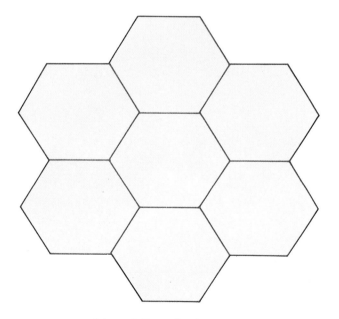

A tessellation using hexagons

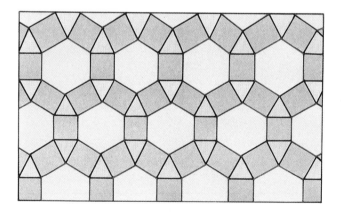

A tessellation using triangles, squares and hexagons

Tessellations using a variety of shapes

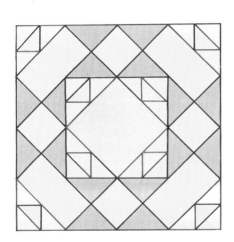

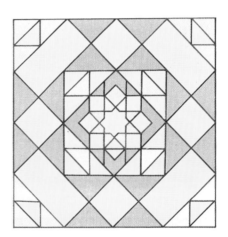

time zone   *noun*

A time zone is a region of the Earth's surface where all the clocks tell the same time. When it is daytime on one side of the Earth, it is night on the other. As travelers move east or west, they pass through different time zones.

There are 24 time zones, and they are counted east or west of Greenwich, in London.

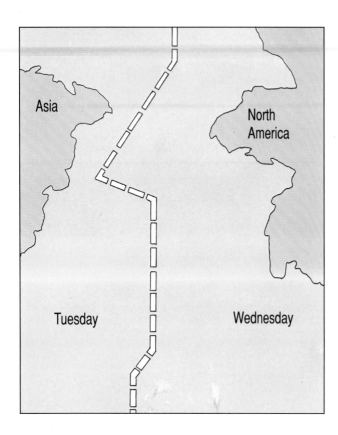

International date line

This imaginary line runs from north to south through the Pacific Ocean. For most of its distance it is exactly halfway around the world from Greenwich. It is where the day's date changes and each new day begins. To the west of the line, it is a day earlier than it is to the east of the line.

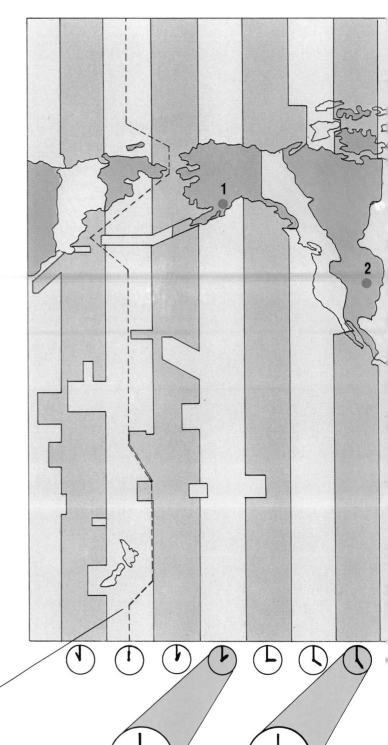

1 In Anchorage, Alaska, it is 2:00 A.M. Everyone is asleep.

2 In Denver, Colorado, it is 5:00 A.M. Early risers are starting to get up.

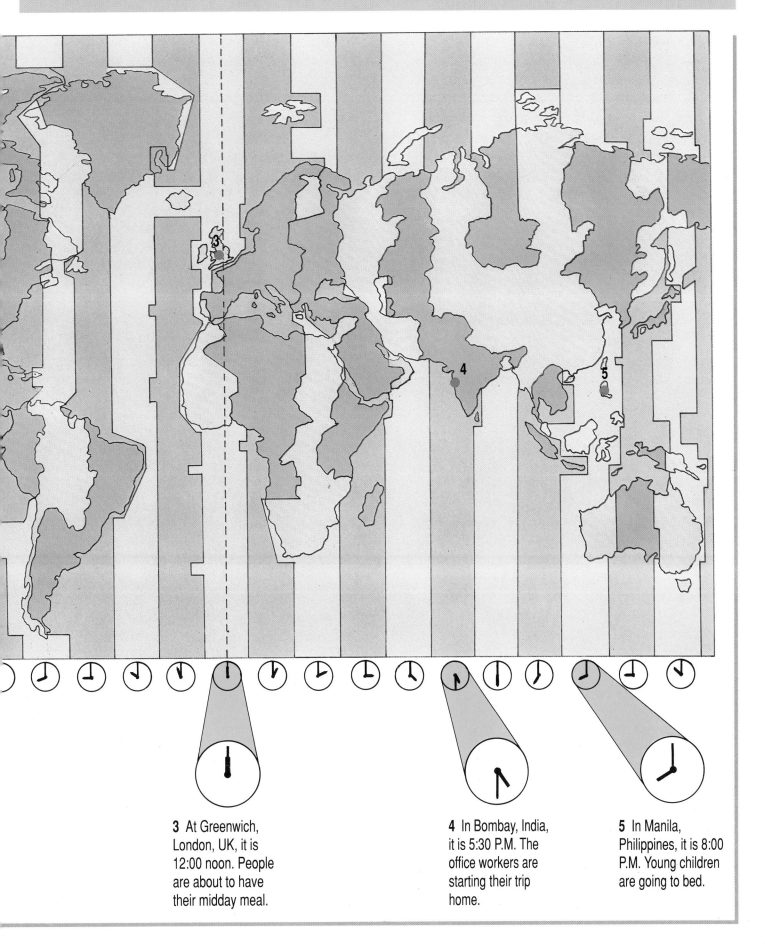

3 At Greenwich, London, UK, it is 12:00 noon. People are about to have their midday meal.

4 In Bombay, India, it is 5:30 P.M. The office workers are starting their trip home.

5 In Manila, Philippines, it is 8:00 P.M. Young children are going to bed.

149

traveler's check   *noun*
A traveler's check is a kind of check used by people who want to spend money in another country where the **currency** is different. To use a traveler's check it must be signed and then given to the foreign bank.
He used a traveler's check to pay for his meal.

treasurer   *noun*
A treasurer is a person who is in charge of **money**.
The club's treasurer told the members how much money the club had.

treasury   *noun*
1. A treasury is a place where **money** and **valuable** objects are kept.
He added $50 to the club's treasury.
2. The treasury is the name sometimes given to the government department that is in charge of the country's **money**.
Taxes are paid to the treasury.

treble   *verb*
To treble means to triple.
The company trebled its sales in one year.

trend   *noun*
A trend is the direction in which something is moving. **Companies** frequently examine the trends in **business** so that they can predict future sales.
The trend is toward higher inflation.

triad   *noun*
A triad is a group of three things.
Every triangle has a triad of angles.

triangle   *noun*
A triangle is a flat **shape** that has three sides. There are four main types of triangles. These are a **right triangle**, an **equilateral triangle**, an **isosceles triangle**, and a **scalene triangle**.
The interior angles of a triangle always add up to 180°.

triangular numbers   *plural noun*
Triangular numbers are **numbers** that form a **triangle** of dots when they are **plotted** on a **graph**. One is the first triangular number and 3 and 6 are the next.
Here are the first four triangular numbers: 1, 3, 6, 10.

trigonometry   *noun*
Trigonometry is the study of the relationship between the **angles** and the sides of **triangles** and other figures. It uses ratios called the **sine**, **cosine** and **tangent**.
He used trigonometry to calculate the angle.

trillion   *noun*
A trillion is equal to one thousand million.
There were more than a billion grains of sand in the box.

trust fund   *noun*
A trust fund is an amount of **money**, **valuables**, or **property** that is set aside for somebody's benefit. For example, it may be set up by parents for their children.
The trust fund ensured that the children would have money to invest when they reached the age of 21.

trustee   *noun*
A trustee is a person who is put in charge of the property or business affairs of another. Some organizations such as hospitals and colleges have boards of trustees who are responsible for handling the business of the institution. **Trust funds** are also administered by trustees.
His aunt was appointed trustee of his affairs until he came of legal age.

twenty-four-hour clock *noun*

The twenty-four-hour clock counts the time straight through from 00:00 hours, or midnight, to 24:00 hours, which is also midnight. Some timetables use twenty-four-hour time. Twenty-four-hour times always have four figures. The first two show the hour, and the last two show the minutes. For example, 04:15 shows that it is 4:15 in the morning, but 16:15 shows that it is 4:15 in the afternoon.

The military uses a twenty-four-hour clock timetable.

This digital clock uses a liquid crystal display face. It uses digits up to 24:00.

The twenty-four-hour clock at Greenwich, England, is unusual. Its hour hand goes around only once every 24 hours.

This clock face has two rings of numbers. It is easy to tell the time using either the 12- or 24-hour system.

The airport terminal clock shows when planes leave and when they arrive. It uses a twenty-four-hour clock so it is easy to tell if the time given is in the morning or afternoon.

turnover *noun*
The turnover of a **business** is the amount of money collected by that business from selling goods and **services** to its customers. Another word for turnover is **sales**.
The turnover of the business increased by $1.5 million last year.

twenty-four-hour clock ► page 151

two-dimensional *adjective*
Two-dimensional describes objects that are flat, such as a piece of paper. Two **coordinates** are needed to locate a **point** on a two-dimensional **surface**. These relate to **length** and width.
A square is a two-dimensional shape.

underwrite *verb*
1. To underwrite is to agree to accept a **financial risk**. Underwriting is done by **insurance companies**, which agree to **pay money** in the event of a disaster.
The insurance company will underwrite his fire insurance policy.
2. To underwrite is to share the risk when a **company** tries to **sell** its **shares** to the public. If the public will not **buy** all of the shares at the required **price**, the underwriting company promises to buy them instead.
A group of insurance companies came together to underwrite the issue of shares in the computer company.
underwriter *noun*

unemployed *adjective*
Unemployed describes people who do not have a **job**. Unemployed people often qualify for payments from the government, this helps them to live while they look for other work. Unemployment can be long-term or temporary.
The number of unemployed workers rose when the factory closed.
unemployment *noun*

union *noun*
The union of two **sets** is the collection of the **members** of both sets into a single set. For example, if a basket of fruit contains a set of apples and a set of oranges, the union of the two sets contains all of the apples and all of the oranges.
The union of two sets can be shown on a Venn diagram.

unit   *noun*

1. A unit is another word for one.
In the decimal system of counting the numbers 1 to 9 are units because they are only one digit long.
2. A unit is a **standard**, or set quantity, of **measurement**. Measuring something is the same as counting the number of units it has. Feet are units of length, and **degrees** are units of angle or temperature.
A gram is a unit of weight.

unearned   *adjective*

Unearned refers to **income** that is not earned by doing work. Unearned income is gotten instead from **profits** on **investments**. The opposite of unearned income is earned income, which includes **salary** and **wages**.
His only unearned income was interest from his bank account.

United States dollar   *noun*

The United States dollar is the **currency** of the United States. There are 100 cents in a dollar.

universal set   *noun*

A universal set describes all the things that need to be included in a particular group because they share at least one **property**. In a library, the universal set is the **set** of all the books on the shelves. These books can be grouped together under different topics, so that each topic forms a **subset** of the universal set of all books.
When we talk about teachers and children, the universal set will be the set of the people in the class.

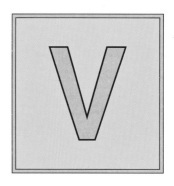

value   *noun*

Value is the worth of something in **money** or **goods**.
The value of the jewelry was $45,000.
valuable   *adjective*
valuables   *plural noun*

variable   *adjective*

Variable is something that changes. The temperature of the sea is a variable because it is warmer in summer than in winter. The opposite of a variable is a **constant**.
The speed of the bus was variable because it kept stopping and starting.

variable   *noun*

In mathematics, a variable is a number or quantity that is unknown. A **symbol**, such as x or y, is used to represent the variable in an **equation**.
In the equation $2x + 1 = 7$, x is the variable.
vary   *verb*

Venn diagram   *noun*

A Venn diagram is a way of drawing **sets** on a piece of paper. Each set is drawn inside a circle or other shape. If the contents of the sets overlap, those things in the overlapping section, or **interset**, can be identified as belonging to both of the sets.

Venn diagrams clearly show the things that are common to two sets.

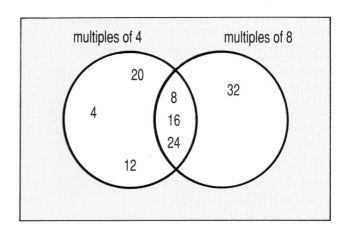

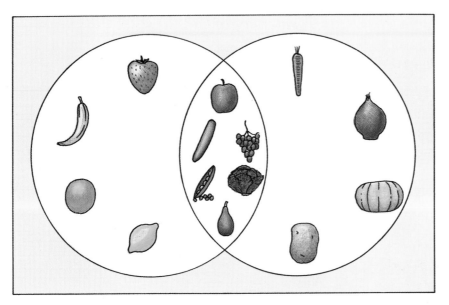

The contents of two sets, one of fruits and one of vegetables, overlap at the interset. The interset contains things common to both sets, in this case things that are green.

The contents of these three sets give four intersets.

1. The orange interset is common to the yellow and red sets.
2. The green interset is common to the yellow and blue sets.
3. The purple interset is common to the red and blue sets.
The dark interset in the middle is common to all 3 sets.

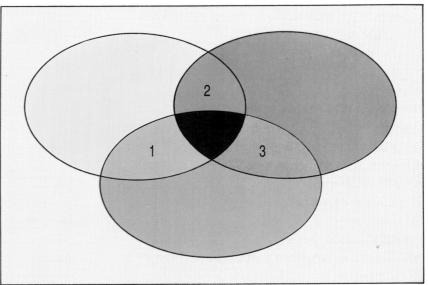

vault *noun*
A vault is a large **safe**. It is used to protect money or **valuables**. Vaults are usually made of steel and are found in **banks**.
The gold was stored in the vault.

vector *noun*
A vector is a **quantity** that shows the **size** and direction of a moving object. The motion of an aircraft is an example of a vector. The speed of the aircraft is illustrated by the size of the vector, and the direction in which the aircraft is traveling is shown by the direction of the vector.
They guided the pilot back to base once they had worked out the plane's vector.

velocity *noun*
Velocity is another word for speed. It is a **measurement** of distance over time. Velocity can be measured in miles per hour, or mph. Velocity is a **vector**.
In order to find the velocity of an object, you divide the distance the object has traveled by the time it took to do so.

Venn diagram ► page 154

venture capital *noun*
Venture capital is **money** that is **borrowed** to start up a new **business**. This money is used for businesses that are expected to make a large **profit**, but there is usually great **risk** as well.
The new movie theatre required venture capital of $200,000.

vertex (plural **vertexes** or **vertices**) *noun*
The vertex is the top, or tip, of a **shape**, or the **point** farthest away from the **base**. The vertex is also the point where two **lines** meet to form an **angle**.
The vertex of a mountain is its peak.

vertical *adjective*
Vertical describes things that point straight up or down.
A flag pole is usually vertical.

volume *noun*
Volume is a **measurement** of the amount of space an object takes up. Some **units** of volume are the **quart** and the **liter**.
Volume is the same as capacity.

voucher *noun*
1. A voucher is a document, or some other written evidence, that a **payment** has been made.
The voucher was evidence enough that the accounts were accurate and true.
2. A voucher is a document that can be exchanged for **goods** or **services**.
Many stores sell gift vouchers, or gift certificates, which can be used instead of money in any of their branches.

vulgar fraction ► **fraction**

wages *plural noun*
Wages are the sums of **money** that an **employee** is **paid** to do a **job**, especially when the pay is figured on an hourly basis.
His wages for mowing the lawn were $5.00 per hour.

Wall Street *noun*
Wall Street is a nickname for the New York Stock Exchange. The stock exchange is situated on Wall Street, in New York City.
The value of shares traded on Wall Street yesterday was unusually high.

wampum *noun*
Wampum refers to beads that were used for **money** by Native Americans. The beads were made from shells and were also used for jewelry. Black shells were more **valuable** than white ones.
She gave him some wampum in exchange for the blanket.

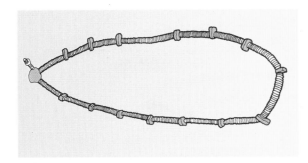

wealth *noun*
Wealth is the **money** and **possessions** that someone owns.
Most of his wealth was invested in his large house.

week *noun*
A week is seven **days**. Many people work for five days of the week and have two days of leisure time. In many countries this rest period is known as the weekend.
It took four weeks to repair the school roof.

weight *noun*
Weight is a **measurement** of the heaviness of something. Two **units** of weight are the **pound** and the **gram**.
The weight of the can was one pound.
weigh *verb*

weights and measures ► page 158

whole number ► integer

wholesale *adjective*
Wholesale describes **goods** that are sold in large **quantities** to **retail stores**. For example, when a shop buys books from a publisher, it **pays** less than the retail **price**. It then **sells** the books at the higher retail price. The difference between the wholesale and retail prices pays for the store's **expenses** and **profits**.
The supermarket bought its fruits and vegetables at a wholesale market.

width *noun*
Width is the wideness, or the distance from side to side, of an object.
The width of the river was 50 feet.

will *noun*
A will is a statement of instructions about the distribution of a person's property after his or her death.
The will stated that his house was to be given to his children.

withdrawal *noun*
Withdrawal is the taking of **money** out of a **bank account**. Usually, only the owner of the account can withdraw money.
He made a withdrawal of $25 from his current account.

World Bank *noun*
The World Bank is an **international bank** that **lends money** to countries for development. It was founded in 1944 to help countries that had been **economically** ruined by the events of World War II.
The World Bank loan helped the country to build essential roads and bridges.

yard *noun*
A yard is an **imperial measure** equal to three **feet**, or 36 inches. It is roughly equal to the **metric length** of 90 **centimeters**.
A yard is approximately the length of a long stride.

year *noun*
A year is the **time** it takes for Earth to travel once around the sun. This is $365\frac{1}{4}$ **days**, so most years are **rounded** down to 365 days. Every four years there is a **leap year**, which has an extra day, February 29th.
The summer Olympic Games are held every four years.

yen *noun*
The yen is the **currency** of Japan.

yield *noun*
The yield is the amount of **money** that is **paid** out on an **investment**. It is sometimes called the return **earned** on an investment.
The yield on their investment was more than they expected.

yuan *noun*
The yuan is the **currency** of China. The yuan is divided into 10 jiao or 100 fen.

157

weights and measures *plural noun*

Weights and measures are **measurements** used to show the size and weight of things. The most commonly used system of measurement in the world is the **metric system**, or SI system. The imperial system is still found, though the metric system has been officially adopted in most countries. *Some of the earliest weights and measures were calculated according to parts of the body, such as the foot or hand.*

	imperial	American
1 pint	0.568 l	0.473 l
1 quart	1.137 l	0.946 l
1 gallon	4.546 l	3.785 l
1 peck (dry)	9.092 l	8.827 l
1 bushel (dry)	36.369 l	35.309 l

The imperial and American systems sometimes use the same terms to mean different amounts.

length and distance

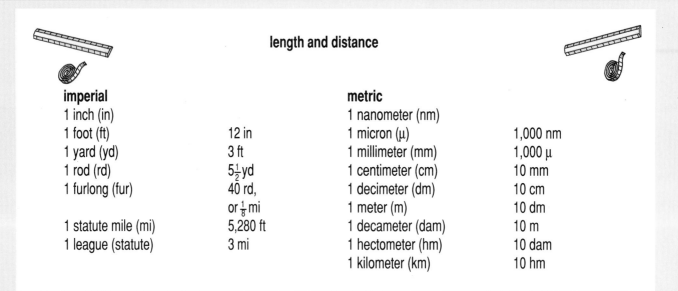

imperial		metric	
1 inch (in)		1 nanometer (nm)	
1 foot (ft)	12 in	1 micron (μ)	1,000 nm
1 yard (yd)	3 ft	1 millimeter (mm)	1,000 μ
1 rod (rd)	$5\frac{1}{2}$ yd	1 centimeter (cm)	10 mm
1 furlong (fur)	40 rd, or $\frac{1}{8}$ mi	1 decimeter (dm)	10 cm
		1 meter (m)	10 dm
1 statute mile (mi)	5,280 ft	1 decameter (dam)	10 m
1 league (statute)	3 mi	1 hectometer (hm)	10 dam
		1 kilometer (km)	10 hm

surface and area

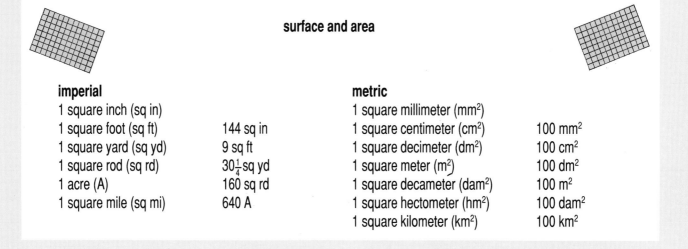

imperial		metric	
1 square inch (sq in)		1 square millimeter (mm²)	
1 square foot (sq ft)	144 sq in	1 square centimeter (cm²)	100 mm²
1 square yard (sq yd)	9 sq ft	1 square decimeter (dm²)	100 cm²
1 square rod (sq rd)	$30\frac{1}{4}$ sq yd	1 square meter (m²)	100 dm²
1 acre (A)	160 sq rd	1 square decameter (dam²)	100 m²
1 square mile (sq mi)	640 A	1 square hectometer (hm²)	100 dam²
		1 square kilometer (km²)	100 km²

volume and capacity

imperial		metric	
1 cubic inch (cu in)		1 cubic millimeter (mm³)	
1 cubic foot (cu ft)	1,728 cu in	1 cubic centimeter (cm³)	1,000 mm³
1 cubic yard (cu yd)	27 cu ft	1 cubic decimeter (dm³)	1,000 cm³
		1 cubic meter (m³)	1,000 dm³
		1 cubic decameter (dam³)	1,000 m³
		1 cubic hectometer (hm³)	1,000 dam³

liquid measure

imperial		metric	
1 fluid dram (fl dr)		1 milliliter (ml)	
1 fluid ounce (fl oz)	8 fl dr	1 centiliter (cl)	10 ml
1 gill (gi)	5 fl oz	1 deciliter (dl)	10 cl
1 pint (pt)	4 gi	1 liter (l)	10 dl
1 quart (qrt)	2 pt	1 decaliter (dal)	10 l
1 gallon (gal)	4 qrt	1 hectoliter (hl)	10 dal
		1 kiloliter (kl)	10 hl

weight and mass

avoirdupois		metric	
1 grain (gr)		1 milligram (mg)	
1 dram (dr)	27.344 grains	1 centigram (cg)	10 mg
1 ounce (oz)	16 drams	1 decigram (dg)	10 cg
1 pound (lb)	16 ounces	1 gram (g)	10 dg
1 stone	14 pounds	1 decagram (dag)	10 g
1 hundredweight (cwt)	100 lbs (American)	1 hectogram (hg)	10 dag
1 hundredweight (cwt)	112 lbs (British)	1 kilogram (kg)	10 hg
1 short ton	2,000 lbs	1 quintal (q)	100 kg
1 long ton	2,240 lbs	1 metric tonne (t)	1,000 kg

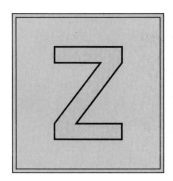

zero *noun*

Zero is the answer obtained when a **number** is **subtracted** from itself. The sign for zero is 0. For example, $7 - 7 = 0$.
Zero is the only number between the positive numbers and the negative numbers.

Zimbabwe dollar *noun*

The Zimbabwe dollar is the **currency** of Zimbabwe. A Zimbabwe dollar is divided into 100 cents.

zloty *noun*

The zloty is the **currency** of Poland. There are 100 groszy in a zloty.